HOW TO WIN
AT
SPORTS
BETTING

HOW TO WIN
AT
SPORTS
BETTING

J. Edward Allen
Gambling Research Institute

First Edition

Library of Congress Catalog Card Number: 90-83813
ISBN: 0-940685-10-8

Gambling Research Institute (GRI) books are published by Cardoza Publishing, the world's foremost publisher of gambling and gaming books. Write for our free catalogue of gambling books, related gaming materials and advanced strategies.

See Back Page for Advanced Strategy Information

CARDOZA PUBLISHING
P.O. Box 1500, Cooper Station
New York, N. Y. 10276

TABLE OF CONTENTS

1. INTRODUCTION

Welcome to the fascinating world of sports betting!

To me, there is no more exciting way to gamble, for it allows you to use all of your skill and knowledge to win money. And if you're good enough, there's no end to the money that can be won. Even better, the sports book can't stop you, and you can't be barred from playing, no matter how much you've taken from the book-maker.

You'll be going one-on-one with the bookmaker, but you can study the situation at your leisure, examine all the important factors, and then make your decision in the privacy of your home! Often, your decision will be to lay off the game, not to bet it. There's no pressure to bet; you pick your own spots!

Although there is no end of excitement in betting on sports events, we're going to show you how to submerge this excitement and have but one goal in mind; winning money, cold, hard cash.

It's fun to win, to come away from the sports book counting that green stuff, feeling all those crisp bills in your hand. That is the true excitement we're going after, and that's the goal of the book, to make you money. And it can be done. It's all here - between the covers.

There is a great fascination with sports in America. Fans live for the seasons, and if their favorite sport is in the limelight, they're in heaven. Some fans love all the sports, and bask in the beauty of that time when football and basketball overlap, or when basketball, football and baseball are all around in the late fall.

I've met a lot of fans in my life. I've met guys who could sprout statistics by the hour. They love the games because of the statistics, which is really an American fascination.

A couple of my close friends have been sports fanatics. Maybe you are also. What really interested me when speaking to these fans was why they didn't put all that knowledge to good use, making money from it. They'd tell me the starting lineups of all major league teams for the last ten years, they'd analyze the strengths and weaknesses of coaches, managers, pitchers, quarterbacks, defenses and offenses. They knew everything, except one thing. That was how to make money from this extensive knowledge.

I've been around the world of gambling for a long time. I've been a pro at various forms of gambling. I've met the top pros, the world champions. It would sound strange, wouldn't it, if a man could tell you the odds in poker, the correct plays in all situations, how to be aggressive, and when to be cautious, when to call and when to raise, when to hold and when to fold, and not play poker? Why then, are all these facts in his head? What is he doing with all that knowledge, if he's not putting it to good use?

And then, why is the sports fan not making money with his knowledge? If he can analyze a game between Dallas and Cleveland in the NFL, figure it all out, weigh the pros and cons of each team, and then figure out roughly who would win and by how much, why isn't he betting the game?

Before I go any further, I want to make clear that I'm not encouraging anyone to gamble. If you are content to be a fan, then be a fan. But I'm presuming that you've picked up this book and are skimming the introduction, or you've already bought the book, so you must have some interest in gambling on sports events.

If you have a little or some or a great deal of knowledge about sports, and want to make money, then read on. We'll deepen your knowledge, we'll show you the winning angles, we'll make a winner out of you.

A great many people find an extra edge in sports if they bet on the games. Millions bet on the World Series in baseball and the Super Bowl in football. It's almost a national pastime to wager on those events. Fewer people bet on games either day in and day out, as in baseball, or week in and week out as in football.

However, the betting that they do runs into the billions of dollars. Yes, you read right and I'm not exaggerating, into the billions of dollars. Unfortunately most of the bettors are losers. But we don't want you to be a loser.

If most of the people who gamble at sports betting are losers, what do they do wrong?

We'll show you in this book. But we're not just going to be negative, and show you what to avoid, we're going to show you the ways to win. Positive ways to win. We're going to show you how to beat the bookie; make him "cry daddy", take his money and put it in to your account, into your pocket!

Above all, in this book, we're going to deal with strategies of winning. This is not a book filled with stats; there are other books and pamphlets and publications loaded with those. They're good for the fans but not for the serious bettors.

What we're going to present in this book are things that will last, that will be as true ten years from now as they are today. We didn't want to write a book that would be out of date a year from now, because the records of the pitchers or teams have changed, or personnel has changed. We understand the fluidity of big time sports personnel and therefore we're not dealing with that factor.

We're going to deal with those timeless principles and strategies of winning that never change, but must be grasped in order to make one a winner.

The games we're going to cover in full, in depth as no other book has ever covered them, is football, both pro and college, basketball, both pro and college, major league baseball, and professional boxing.

For each individual sport, we'll also show the teams invlolved and the leagues they play in (with the exception of boxing, an individual sport). We'll show you the various ways you can wager on sports events and make money from each of those ways. We'll show you how to avoid sucker and trap plays which can quickly drain any bankroll.

We'll not only deal with the sports but with methods of preserving capital and correct money management, which can be just as important as picking the right team.

We'll start at the beginning and go through every phase of sports betting. Not only will we show you how to study and interpert a line, we'll show you the rationale behind the line. We'll dig deeper than any book has dug before. At every point, you'll know what is in the bookie's head, so that you can outwit and outsmart him, and make money as a result.

So let us now begin. Our next chapter will deal with the principles of winning at sports betting, no matter what the sport.

It's time for us to get ready to cash in those winning tickets!

2. THE PRINCIPLES OF WINNING AT SPORTS BETTING

Some of the principles that we'll mention will overlap, but don't worry about that. The important thing is to study this section and the principles that we outline, for that will have a positive impact in your pocketbook; it will get bigger and fatter!

1. Bet on sports events to make money, and for that one reason only!

That sounds pretty ordinary and logical, but you'd be surprised at how many people gamble for all the wrong reasons. A lot of betting action comes from men and women who gamble for the thrill of it, for the excitement of making a wager that may lose.

Remember this and remember it well The most exciting part of gambling on sports events is cashing in that winning ticket, getting that MOOLAH in your hands. Otherwise you're mixing up excitement with anxiety.

Forget about the games on TV if there's no edge there for you to make money. Do other things that bring excitement to your life. You would never think of going to a bank with a cash deposit and throwing the money up in the air, hoping you wouldn't lose any in the wind. There's excitement in that, and plenty of anxiety as well. But you'd have to be a fool to do it.

2. Bet only on those games or events where you have the best chance of winning.

Bet to win. Pick out those games you've analyzed where you

have the edge over the bookie, where you know more than he does, where you have the superior insight. Otherwise don't bet.

Many bettors make bets in baseball, where there's action from morning to night. For example, if they live on the West Coast, they're betting on a game played in the East, so that results are coming in by mid-morning. Then they bet on a game in the Mid-west for the afternoon results, then a West Coast team for the late afternoon results, then a night game somewhere in the country to keep them going to the wee hours of the morning.

All they want is action, but that kind of mindless gambling is going to hit them in the pocketbook. Betting shouldn't be for enter-tainment, something to pass away the time. It's too expensive and can be dangerous when betting gets out of hand. Pick your spots, and bet only on games that you've analyzed. Get that into your head, or you won't be a winner.

3. Bet with your head, not with your heart.

Another way of saying this is, don't disregard the facts because of emotional attachments. For example, there are a great many bettors who follow one particular team fanatically, and bet on that team no matter what the situation.

There are people in Indiana who bet UI (University of Indiana) in basketball because they're basketball crazy, and Indiana is the team representing their state. That's foolish, because Indiana may have a bad season, or Indiana may have a winning season and be penalized by the bookies. If a fan bets on Bobby Knight's team blindly, he's going to lose money.

This concept doesn't just extend to team sports. A perfect ex-ample of bettors wagering with their heart was the Muhammed Ali-Larry Holmes fight. Ali was old and washed up by this fight, while Holmes was a strong younger bull, undefeated as a fighter. Yet the odds were in favor of Holmes by only 8-5.

An astute gambler who I respected very much told me that Holmes should have been 6-1 or even an 8-1 favorite. Why wasn't he? Because all those Ali fans, who had been thrilled by his per-formances over the years, kept pushing in the money on Ali. It wasn't even a contest.

4. Don't be a fan.

If you're betting seriously, you can't afford to be a fan. If you're a fan you're following one team, and you may close your mind to other teams. If you're a Yankee fan, you may know their lineup inside out, but you can't bet against them, even when you know they're overmatched. How can you bet against your beloved Yankees? And while you're concentrating on the Bronx Bombers, you're overlooking terrific plays on other teams, plays that could earn you big money.

You have to get away from this concept of being a fan to make money. The reason that 95% of bettors on sports events lose money is, among other reasons, their blind allegiance to individual teams. Take a cold viewpoint of the sport you're betting on. all teams should be alike to you emotionally.

5. Betting money on a team doesn't help the team.

Out of loyalty to a particular team, a gambler makes a big bet. But the team doesn't know about the bet, and it doesn't help the team. even if the players knew that Joe Nobody had bet $100 on them to beat another team, what difference is it going to make? None at all.

Showing this kind of loyalty to your team, being true to your team makes no difference at all, except in your pocketbook. Hero worship and team worship doesn't make money for anyone except the players. Those who worship have to pay!

If you want to collect the star's autograph, and it costs you $5, at least you have the baseball card. But shelling out $110 to a bookie and losing that bet gets you nothing.

6. Pay attention to money management

There are several bettors that I know who win a lot of bets and end up losing money. How can they accomplish this? It's easy. They're betting incorrectly. For example, during football season, they win four $100 bets and lose one $500 bet, so, even winning four out of five games on a weekend, they're down the drain over $100 (counting the bookie's vigorish edge).

Study the sections on money management and learn how to make use of your bankroll for optimum effect. You'll learn just what percentage of that bankroll should be bet on any one game.

7. Forget about touts and tipsters.

During any sports season there will be plenty of ads in the sports pages, and in various periodicals, telling you how some individual or organization is going to make a fortune for you if you listen to their tips. If you do decide to listen to them, all you'll do is dent your bankroll.

I've forgotten how many times I've read about the "lock of the year, " or "Lock of the decade." A "lock" to the unitiated, is a "sure thing", a "can't miss" situation. Well, if the tout has a sure thing, why isn't he betting his own bankroll on it, and getting rich?

What does he need your paltry fee of $50 or whatever fee he charges to tell you about it?

It's so logical that most people can't understand it, so they send away money to the touts or call them and give away money they'd best keep.

Some touts give you a sure-fire winner but only if you call twice. For example, team A is playing team B, and the tout, in his newspaper or magazine ad, is screaming about the "lock of the decade."

Well, I call him up and he gives me team A. An hour later later I call him up using a different name gives me team B. Of course, I have to lose money betting on both teams, but half his callers are going to believe in him, and half are going to lose money.

It's a can't miss situation for the tout, and a can't win situation for his followers.

8. Keep a cool head

No matter how astute the bettor, he or she is bound to have a losing steak. It's the very nature of the game. The sports teams you're betting on are made up of men, and men can make mistakes. No matter how well team A looks, if their return man fumbles the kickoff, and you've bet on that team, you're in trouble. Suddenly your team has to play catch up ball and ends up going against its own winning strategy.

Or a pitcher's arm is injured, or the star guard on the basketball team comes down with a hamstring injury. These things happen all the time, and upset your winning formula. Suddenly you've lost five games in a row. What do you do?

Keep a cool head. Rethink your analysis of the game or games you've lost. Stop betting for awhile, and make only mind bets. If you start winning again, bet real money, but if your losing streak continues, restudy your line or analysis of the game. Until you straighten this out, don't bet real cash.

If you follow these eight principles, you're already way ahead of the game. You're doing what 95% of the gamblers on sports events refuse to do. You're now on your way to becoming a winner!

HOW TO WIN AT SPORTS BETTING

3. Pro Football
A. Betting on the NFL Games

Professional football as played in the National Football League, the NFL, has captured the imagination of American sports fans, but it wasn't always this way. The League was formed in the 1920s with pioneers such as George Halas leading the way, and the franchises went to wherever there was sponsorship. Teams relied on one big star attraction, such as Red Grange, to draw in the crowds.

All this changed with the advent of television, which discovered an ideal broadcasting vehicle in the pro football games. The play was rather leisurely for the camera, for unlike soccer or hockey, where the action is almost nonstop, here there were intervals between plays, and further intervals when a team made a first down.

And the action for the most part could be narrowed down to what the quarterback did. If he handed the ball off for a run, that was easily covered. If it was a passing play, the camera picked it up quickly.

When millions of fans could see the game on the tube in their home or at a bar, the pro game really took off in popularity. And there were other changes as well. Except for Green Bay, which held one of the early franchises, all of the franchises were in major television markets with broad population bases to support the teams.

Franchises in the NFL are worth millions of dollars, running over a hundred million in several cases. It is big-time as only American sports can be big-time, with special viewing boxes in many stadiums for multi-millionaire fans, with all the hoopla of a

Super Bowl, with the stars commanding huge salaries and terrific recognition.

It is also a terrific betting vehicle. The games are generally played on Sunday during the season, except for the Monday night games, which have been around for years and are a national institution. Some games are played on Saturday late in the season when the college games have ended.

But for most Americans, Sunday is a time to sit down before the TV set and watch the games being broadcast. The market determines the games, and if the game is sold out, it may be shown in the home market. Otherwise other games are shown.

There is generally a morning game and an afternoon game, depending on the location of the viewer. On the West Coast, the games usually come on at 10 AM and 1 PM; in the East, with a three hour difference, the afternoon game can begin at 4 PM.

From the time television discovered pro football, it has become a great betting vehicle. Millions of fans form a solid base of gamblers, who wager either a friendly bet with other friends or more seriously bet on the outcome with illegal bookmakers. But whether legal or illegal, millions of dollars are bet on the NFL games each weekend.

Certainly, having a bet on the game allows the viewer to have a stronger interest in the outcome of the game, and this has also helped swell the popularity of NFL games. And the more games shown on television, the more action the bookies receive. A lot of people like to bet on games they can watch, and restrict themselves to gambling on those games alone.

If Green Bay is playing Minnesota on national TV, there will be a lot of action on that game all over the country. The Monday night games on ABC also promote a tremendous amount of action. Wherever the American people are, if they can see the game, they'll bet on it.

Television gives the viewers a unique look at pro football. Not only is the action covered, but there are things like "instant replay", where the previous play is shown over again, often several times from different angles. The viewer can easily see what happened, and who made the good play and who screwed it up. From this close-up range they can study the various players on the teams and make judgments as to their respective abilities. The fans get to know players from practically all the teams in this way.

With this added knowledge, intimately discovered through the television tube, fans become bettors, feeling that they can weigh the next game. And the bookmakers happily accommodate them. Pro football's bettors all have a **pointspread line**, or simply ,**the line,** as the basis for their wagers.

This line makes one team a favorite over another by a number of points. If you like the underdog, you receive points; if you want to bet on the favorite, you have to give points. It's as simple as that. And it becomes a very attractive lure for bettors.

Since the heart of all action is the spread, let's start our discussion of pro football betting by showing how it works, and going deeper, analyze the factors that determine the spread. We'll also find out the real and true purpose of the pointspread, who makes it, how it may differ from region to region.

THE POINTSPREAD

In practically all of the games played in the NFL, one team is favored over another. As we mentioned before, if you want to bet on the favorite, you have to give points; if you bet on the underdog, you get points. Let's give an example of this.

Suppose that Green Bay is playing Minnesota at Green Bay. This particular year, Minnesota has a very strong team and Green Bay a mediocre one. If the bookmaker allowed all of the bettors to select a team to bet on without anyone being penalized by giving or laying points, the overwhelming decision by gamblers would be to bet on Minnesota.

Minnesota, on the basis of team strength, should win the game. There would be a few die-hard fans of Green Bay that would bet on Green Bay, but these kinds of fools are few and far between. Still, there are fans that might blindly do this. That's why, in one of my principles of winning, I mentioned that you cannot be a fan and expect to win money betting on pro football, if being a fan colors your judgment.

Now, the bookmakers could do what they do in boxing, and

make Minnesota a 2-1 favorite, or maybe a 3-1 favorite to win the game. In that case, if you favored Minnesota, you'd have to lay the odds. You'd have to bet either $2 or $3 to win $1. But since Minnesota is considered, for this example, the much stronger team, there would still be an imbalance of money bet on the Vikings.

However, the bookmakers know that if they make the Vikings favorites by a certain number of points, then money would go both ways. Some gamblers would bet on Minnesota, laying or giving the points, while a practically equal number would go the other way and take or accept the points and bet on the Green Bay Packers.

But what number would be correct?

That number which is selected, the points by which one team is favored over another, is the **pointspread** and is an art form in itself.

Most gamblers think that the number picked shows the relative strength of the two teams, and if Minnesota is a 10 point favorite over Green Bay, then the bookmakers think that Minnesota is in reality 10 points stronger than Green Bay. But that's not the case at all. And if you see the reasoning behind the pointspread you will have an extra insight into betting on pro football that will stand you in very good stead when you select a team to bet on.

The pointspread is formulated to get *equal* betting action, so that the bookmaker can make a living. When you bet on NFL games you have to lay 11-10 with the bookie. This means that a $10 bet costs you $11.

Thus, if you win one game laying $11-10 and lose one at $11-10, you've ended up losing $1. When a bookie gets equal action on both sides of the same bet, he makes his profit the same way. One side loses $11 and the other side wins $10, and the bookie has a $1 profit. When it runs into thousands of dollars bet equally on both sides, the bookie's profit is so much greater.

The actual score of the game is the **straight-up** score, but this isn't important to the bettor. What is important is that he covers the spread. If Minnesota is favored by 10 points over Green Bay, and wins by 11 or more, and he bet on Minnesota, Minnesota covered the spread, and he wins his bet.

If Minnesota won by 9 points or less or lost outright (straight-up), then Minnesota didn't cover the spread and the gambler loses his bet.

If he bet on the underdog, Green Bay, he doesn't care if Green Bay lost the game straight-up, as long as they covered. For example, if the final score is Minnesota 21 - Green Bay 17 and the bettor received 10 points, Green Bay has covered, and he's won his bet.

What if the game falls on the number, with Minnesota, favored by 10, winning by 10?

Then it's a push, with neither the bettor or bookie winning his bet or losing it. The money has to be returned by the bookie to the gambler. That's why bookies hate pushes and don't want the score to be exactly on the number selected in the pointspread.

Now we can see that the line doesn't reflect the exact relative strength of the two teams, only an approximate strength. Now, let's see how this is done.

Football has a peculiar scoring system. Unlike other games, such as baseball, soccer or hockey, where each score is given one point's value, in football the most frequent score, **a touchdown (TD)**, is awarded 6 points. Then the **point-after** is given an additional 1 point.

The most common score resulting from a touchdown is 7 points, allowing 6 for the TD and one for the point-after, which is almost automatic in pro football.

The next most frequent point total is 3 points, when a team kicks **a field goal (FG)**, the least frequent score is 2 points, when a team scores a **safety**. That is almost a negligible concept in pro football, even though it happens a few times a season.

Therefore, the scores that a bookmaker and bettor have to contend with most of the time is the 7 points for TD and point after and a 3 point FG.

Most NFL scores, in fact, practically all of them reflect this distribution of points. Scores are 21-3, 10-7 and so forth. Occasionally a missed point after alters the score, so that one team wins 14-13, the 13 points showing two touchdowns, but one point after missed.

Since the game is played by these multiples of points, the oddsmaker, the person who makes the line, might make the pointspread reflect a score where there cannot be a push. For example, instead of making one team a 10 point favorite, he might make that team an 11 point favorite.

Now, it's going to be extremely difficult for a push to result. Of course , the danger in this line of reasoning, as far as the book-maker is concerned, is that an 11 point favorite might as well be a 13 point favorite, because there is no one point scoring, and 2 point scoring is rare. What happens then is that a load of money goes over to the underdog because there's too many points that the fa-vorite must score to cover the spread and win money for the bettors on the favored team.

Another, surer method the bookmakers use, is to make one team a favorite over the other in half-points. For example, if Minnesota is a 9 1/2 point favorite over Green Bay, there can be no push, for there's no 1/2 point in football. However, both of these methods, the very odd number, such as 11, or the 1/2 point, aren't used that often. Because now we come to a crucial concept in formulating the line. I'm going to highlight it because of it's importance.

The line is made up for the bookmaker's use, not for the betting public. The line is made up so that money flows equally to both sides, the favorite and the underdog.

That, in a nutshell, is what the line is all about. Now that we understand this, we can now see the factors going into the pointspread.

First of all, as noted before, the relative strengths of the teams. That factor must be taken into consideration. In practically all situ-ations, **the favorite** is regarded as the strongest team in terms of talent.

Secondly, the **home field advantage**. When a team plays at home, it has a definite advantage. It is playing on a field it's famil-iar with, in front of its home town fans. It has its rooters and supporters there, usually 60,000 to 80,000 strong. These vocal fans influence not only a home town's team's play, but the officials. Calls that can go either way, usually go against the visiting team. No point in antagonizing the home fans. This is not even done consciously but becomes a definite factor.

Teams usually play better at home, with more incentive. They're on familiar ground, before their loyal fans. They may be more rested, having practiced at the home field all week. They didn't have to fly in the day before. The reasons go on and on.

Bookmakers and oddsmakers recognize this and usually assign 3 points to the team playing at home for the home field advantage, or **HFA**.

When a line is shown in the local newspaper, the universal method of showing which team is at home is to show the team in capital letters. Thus, our example of Minnesota - Green Bay, with Green Bay playing at home, would be shown as follows:

Minnesota - GREEN BAY +10

We see that Minnesota is the favorite, for it is mentioned first. Green Bay is at home because it is in caps. The +10 shows that Green Bay is the underdog by 10 points. Sometimes a -10 will be shown. For example, the line may simply show:

Minnesota -10   GREEN BAY

It's the very same thing. Minnesota's -10 shows that the Vikings are 10 point favorites.

The third factor that the bookmakers take into consideration is - how does the betting public view this game?

As in the stock market, the betting public is generally wrong. 95% of all bettors on sports events are losers , and that goes for pro football. If the bookmakers sense that the public views Green Bay as strong because of an upset win the previous week, they will alter the spread, giving Green Bay a couple of extra points in the spread.

For example, If Green Bay upset the Chicago Bears the previous week, even though they're still much weaker than Minnesota, the line might be Green Bay +8. Here the odd number 8 doesn't really matter. It's just an enticement to a lot of bettors to bet Green Bay. The bookmakers aren't worried that money will swing over to Minnesota because of the lowered pointspread, because they know the public thinks that Green Bay is strong and money will flow to Green Bay anyway.

This often happens, and the most glaring example of all is the 1968 Super Bowl game between the New York Jets and the Baltimore Colts, where the betting public saw the Colts, with their proud dynasty on the line, as a much stronger team than Joe Na-math's upstart Jets. The Colts were installed as 17 point favorites because that's the way the betting public perceived the game. Those on the inside felt that the Jets were a stronger team.

What could have happened if the Jets were made favorites in that game? Tons of money would have gone on the Colts and nothing much on the Jets. When this happens, the bookmakers are now gambling, not the bettors.

To make a bookmaker happy, money should go equally on both sides. In this way, he's assured of a profit, as we saw before with the $11 examples.

But when he's **sided,** that is , when money pours in on one side to the detriment of the other, he's in trouble. He may have to lay off the extra money with other bookies, cutting his profit, or he may just have to gamble.

Therefore, the public's *perception* of the relative strengths of the two teams cannot be underestimated, and in reality isn't by the oddsmakers and the bookmakers.

What they know which the betting public doesn't, is that the game is played by pros, and one bad week, or one good week doesn't make a season. A good team that's upset one week is still good, and a bad team that's upset a stronger team, is still bad.

If you remember this concept, it will make you money and save you from "trap" situations, where you fall into a trap on just one week's random performance by a team that either played over its heads or below its real strength.

The final factor in determining the makeup of the pointspread is "where's the money coming from?"

What this means is - on what team is the heavy money going to be bet?

For example, there's more money in Los Angeles than there is in Pittsburgh. Not only is Los Angeles a richer area, but there are more millionaires there, more people with new money, more action guys, more gamblers and it's close to Vegas. Pittsburgh may have a proud tradition in the NFL but its in the rustbelt of America. There's some old money there, but basically it's a blue collar town.

The Los Angelinos have money burning in their pockets and

they love the Rams and want to support them with action. Well, the bookmakers know this full well. Not only do gamblers from Los Angeles want to bet big money, but they often head for Vegas on the weekends to plunk down cold cash on the Rams. If all that money is coming down on the Rams and the LA team is playing the Pittsburgh Steelers, well, the oddsmakers figure, we can penalize the LA bettors. They'll bet anyway. And we also have to entice the money that wouldn't ordinarily go on Pittsburgh.

Let's suppose that the Rams are at Pittsburgh, and it's going to be a nationally televised game, with the huge LA and Southern California TV market set for this game. Let's assume that the Rams are a better team this year, but have had a few injuries, so that in reality, they may be one touchdown better. If we take away from that the 3 point home field advantage for the Steelers, then an ideal number might be the Rams favored by 4 points.

However, the oddsmakers know that tons of money is just waiting to be bet on the Rams anyway, so if they post the following line:

Los Angeles - PITTSBURGH +4

The bookmakers will be sided, with five dollars going on the Rams for every dollar on the Steelers. So what are the oddsmakers to do? Simple - they make the Rams 7 point favorites, in effect penalizing the exuberant Rams' bettors. Now the official line reads:

Los Angeles - PITTSBURGH +7

And now money starts coming in on Pittsburgh. After all, astute bettors will realize, the Rams aren't that much better, and anyway the game is being played at Pittsburgh.

Another kind of team that's penalized is the "national team.". This is an odd concept because in effect, there is no national team that represents all of America. For many years, the Dallas Cowboys liked to bill themselves as "America's team", and they got money support from all over the country.

In their heyday, running to the middle of the 1980's, the Cowboys were often penalized in the pointspread, because money was always going to be bet on that Dallas team from all over the country, they were America's darlings, with movies made about their cheerleaders, for example.

National teams change from year to year, depending on the fickle public. Usually it's the team that showed Super Bowl winning strength the year before. One year it was Chicago, then the New York Giants, then the San Francisco 49ers.

It's something that passes as quickly as other fads. Usually, it's best to bet against national teams, teams that are favored all over the country, because the oddsmakers are punishing their supporters in the pointspread.

Thus far, we've talked about situations where one team is favored over the other. What happens if the oddsmaker decides that neither team deserves to be a favorite?

In that case, the game is marked as **Pick'Em**. No matter which team you bet on, you're not giving or receiving points. You still have to bet $11 to win $10, on either side.

BALANCING THE BOOKS

Now we come to a situation where, for one reason or another, the points put up on the board aren't correct as far as the betting public is concerned. Let's assume another hypothetical situation. Tampa Bay is playing at home against New Orleans, and the bookmakers have established New Orleans as -1, that is, a one point favorite. The line is put up, and the betting now commences in Vegas legally, and illegally around the country.

From the outset, the bookies realize that they're getting "sided,", that money is pouring in on New Orleans, and they're getting no action on Tampa. Well, how are they going to balance their books, so to speak?

They raise the points. They make New Orleans a 2 point favorite and the next day the papers read:

New Orleans - TAMPA BAY +2

But that doesn't stem the tide. The bookies raise the points to 3 and then 4 and then, by the end of the week the game may read:

New Orleans - TAMPA BAY +6 1/2

By this time, they've enticed a lot of money to go on the Bucs from Tampa Bay. After all 6 1/2 points is a lot more than 1 point

This situation happens during a season, and the astute bettor should watch it carefully. What's really going on? Perhaps the big bettors, the really high rollers, have some kind of inside information. Maybe there's a nagging injury among a couple of key players on the Bucs. Maybe there's a drug problem that's about to explode. Maybe the Saints are looking really sharp and have a strong psychological motivation to win the game. Or maybe it's nothing at all, just a wrong number put up by the oddsmaker. Whatever it is, watch these powerful changes in the line.

We've shown how a pointspread can change, and a question often asked is this - if I bet on a game and bet the favorite and had to lay 1 point, and later on the favorite gets stronger and now is a 61/2 point favorite, does my bet reflect the -1 or the -61/2?

In other words how many points does my team have to win by for me to cash in my bet?

The answer is this - when you make your bet and lay your points, those are the exact points your bet is bound by. If you laid one point, your team has to win by more than one point for you to have a winner. If your team wins by exactly one point, it's a push. If your team ties the game or loses straight-up, you lose your bet.

Now, there may come a situation where you've made several bets on the same game. You've bet on the favorite and laid one point, then made a later bet and laid three points, and finally you've laid four points on the same game.

Let's assume you've bet $110-100 at one point, $55-50 at 3 points, and $33-30 at four points. The final score is Your Team 23 - Opponent 20. What have you won and lost?

First of all you've won $100 for the $110 bet. The bookie will give you back $210, representing $110 for your bet and $100 in winnings. Since your team won by three points, your three point bet is a push and you're given back $55. No win or loss. However, your laying of four points has lost, and you lose your $33. Your total win is $67.

OTHER CHANGES IN THE LINE

Even though there's an official line coming out of Las Vegas, which determines the pointspread around the country, bookmakers in particular cities may have trouble with the line. Often, in cities where there's an NFL team, there's a tremendous amount of action on that team, out of proportion to its actual strength.

The bookies in that city are often in danger of being sided by the rabid fans who bet on pro football. Let's look at another theoretical example of this:

Let's assume that the Dallas Cowboys are playing the Miami Dolphins at Miami, and Miami has been established as a 3 point favorite, mainly because of the home field advantage they have in Joe Robbie Stadium. There's money in Southern Florida and it's been coming in steadily on the Dolphins there, with very little on Dallas. So, to balance the books, the bookmakers run the following line in Miami and southern Florida:

MIAMI - Dallas +4

That extra point means an awful lot, because, as we know, football is a game of 3 points and 7 points primarily, and the 4 point spread means that Miami will need another score to win the game, either a field goal or a touchdown. They won't find one point scores anywhere. So now, in Miami, the bettors are pausing and thinking, hey, Dallas has a chance here, and money goes on Dallas.

At the same time, there's a lot of action in Dallas and the surrounding territory. After all, this is gambling country, action country, where millions have been made by wildcatters in the oil fields. These people are used to a gamble. Money comes in on Dallas, and not too much is coming in on Miami. So the line in Dallas may look like this:

MIAMI - Dallas +2

Now the bettors in the Dallas are thinking that Miami at home looks pretty good here. They're only 2 point favorites, even less than the home field advantage, and all they have to do is win by a field goal to cover the spread. So money starts coming in on Miami.

In essence what is happening is that the home team's bettors are getting penalized slightly by the bookies. But don't think that these one-point differentials don't mean much. In the course of a season, they may mean the difference between a few wins or a few losses. Many of the pros I know, the really smart gamblers, are always "shopping for value". They look for that extra point or two, for it pays off in winning bets. And you should also.

One smart way is to go against the grain in a city you live in. If you feel that the home team should be bet against, then do it for value at home. That's why the concept of being a "fan" is so destructive. You're giving away money by being a fan.

Another important factor, which I have observed happening season after season is this - as the week moves along from Tuesday to gametime, the favorite has a tendency to get stronger and the underdog weaker, as far as the spread is concerned.

Let's show this by another hypothetical situation. Let's assume that Cleveland is playing at home against Detroit. The Cleveland Browns have been established as a 6 point favorite.

CLEVELAND - Detroit +6

This line remains the same from Tuesday through Friday, but on Saturday it changes to Cleveland being favorites by 6 1/2, and then by late Saturday night, Cleveland is quoted at -7. A whole point has moved in the game, and we know how important one whole point is over the course of a season.

What has happened? Has Cleveland gotten stronger talent-wise during the week? Has Detroit weakened? Not necessarily. It's a sheep follow sheep syndrome that often is seen at a racetrack, where last minute betting drops the favorite down from 8-5 to 7-5.

What it generally means is that the bettors, not having made up their minds as to a particular game, go with the favorite. After all, it's a better team, isn't it, or it wouldn't be a favorite? So they plunk their money down on the better teams and run from the weaker dogs.

This happens over and over again at the racetrack, where the gamblers stare blankly at the Racing Form, not able to see anything worth betting on, and then, desperate, they go to the favorite. After all, if the horse is a favorite, it must be the best, right? Of course, favorites at the race track come in only about 34% of the time, so making this type of bet is statistically, 66% incorrect.

It's a bit different betting on the favorite in the NFL.

You're not going to be wrong 66% of the time, but you have to be right more than 50% of the time, otherwise you'll be losing money. And giving away these extra points only hurts you, if you bet on the favorites late in the week. You want and edge at all times, and instead you're giving away the edge.

To take advantage of the extra points possible, and get the edge, do the following: If you bet the favorite, bet it early in the week. If you bet the underdog, do it late in the week.

That's getting value!

It makes a big difference between laying 6 and laying 7 points betting the favorite. And it makes just as big a difference getting 7 instead of 6 points betting on the underdog.

Value! Shop for it at all times in the big store that is NFL betting. Don't overpay for anything. Get bargains. Get things on the cheap. Be smart.

THE OFFICIAL LINE OUT OF VEGAS

Nevada is the only state that permits legal betting on sports events, and in its largest city, Las Vegas, the official line on pro football is made. Oddsmakers have changed over the years. At one time it was Bob Martin, the astute and legendary figure. Today it is Roxy Rosborough. Tomorrow it might be someone else.

But whoever it is, the man making the line, the oddsmaker, knows what he is doing.

It is an awesome responsibility, for millions of dollars ride on the numbers coming out of Las Vegas. A whole underground economy is dependent upon those numbers, and literally millions of people study the line, looking for a spot for their money.

As any of you know who have examined the line, it is tight, very tight. The numbers shown are so relevant that it becomes difficult to decide which way to bet, whether to go with the favorite or wager on the underdog. The line is made, as we have seen, to attract action on both sides, to allow the bookmaker to take in his profits.

I've seen amateurs attempt to pick winners by betting all the games shown. Generally, they've scored way down in the 40% winning range. It's tough to find what are known as "creases" in the official line coming out of Las Vegas. By **creases**, I mean mistakes in the line, spots where you have taken advantage of ignorance on the part of the oddsmakers.

Remember, you're not dealing with a bunch of yo-yos pulling

numbers out of their hats or the thin air; you're dealing with the very best in the profession upon whose opinions millions of dollars are wagered and won and lost each week. You've got to be smarter than they are to beat them.

That can be done. We've already shown you several ways in which the line can be distorted. You must take advantage of these distortions, such as home team penalties in the pointspread, misconceptions by the public and so forth.

As we go along in this chapter, we'll show you what to look for and how to take advantage of these lucrative situations. We'll show you how to beat the spread.

Since the vast majority of the NFL games are played on Sunday, by Monday the oddsmakers are working on the next week's line. It's formed Monday, and discussed and gone over by the experts in Vegas and by Monday night it's ready to be sent out so that most daily newspapers around the country have it. The betting public usually has from Wednesday till early Sunday morning to digest the numbers and make their decisions.

Many times the line will stay pretty rigid. There will be hardly any deviation. However, there are certain changes that we have already shown causing a change in the line during the week. These could be outlined as follows:

A. Penalizing the home team so that money flows the other way.

B. Money moving in one direction so that the line must be changed to balance the books.

C. The tendency for favorite to get stronger as the week progresses.

Take advantage of these three factors and you're already way ahead of the game. Get those extra points and they'll add up to a winning season, all other things being equal.

THE BOOKMAKER'S ADVANTAGE

We've seen how betting with the bookmaker forces the gambler to lay 11-10 on all bets. Thus, a $10 bet becomes $11, a $20 bet, $22 and so forth. That extra 10% is what gives the bookmaker his advantage, and it is expressed as **vigorish** or **vig**.

Just how much is that vig?

With the 11-10 bet, he is giving the bookmaker an edge of 4.54%. Here's how this is figured.

A straight 11-10 adding a dollar to 10 dollars, is a disadvantage of 9.09%. However, since the bettor is expected theoretically to win half his games and lose the other half, that figure is halved down to 4.54%.

This is the bookie's vig, **4.54%**, and a number familiar, or one that should be familiar, to all bettors on pro football.

It doesn't matter whether or not you bet on the favorite or the underdog, on any pick'em situation - the bookmaker is going to collect that vig from you.

You can readily see that being right 50% of the time , isn't going to do anything but lose you money. Let's see why. Suppose you bet $110-100 on six games on a particular Sunday, and won three and lost three. Here's how you'd end up.

```
Three losses at $110 each = -$330
Three wins at $100 each   = -$300
Net result                = -  30
```

If you can't win at least 50% of the time, then it gets more damaging to your bankbook.

```
Four losses at $110 each   =-$440
Two wins at $100 each      =+$200
Net result                 =-$240
```

With the bookies' vig working all the time, we're going to have to be smarter than he is to beat him. That's the purpose of this book, to show you how to win enough times to overcome the vig and come out ahead.

Just what percentage of times do you have to win in order to break even?

The answer is 52.38% of the time.

Along with the 4.54% vig this number, 52.38% should always

remain in your consciousness. It's an important number.

This vig, this extra percentage that the bookie has going for him has been the downfall of many a person betting sports events. We must overcome it to come out ahead. It can be done. It has been done year after year by top pros. And you can do it also. As you read along, we'll show you how.

The Over and Under Bet

Thus far we've discussed betting teams strictly on the pointspread, deciding which team, the favorite or the underdog, warrants our bet. Either way, we have to lay 11-10. However, there are other ways to bet on pro football, and one of the most popular is the Over and Under Bet.

When we make this bet, we're not interested in who wins or loses the game. That doesn't matter at all. What we want to know is the final total of points scored in the game, adding them all up.

For example if the final score is NY Jets 42 Buffalo 16, then their total points scored is 58 (42+16). That is the important number. We couldn't care less if Buffalo has scored the 42 points and the Jets the 16 points. Remember, we can't be bothered about who wins and loses, just the points they pile up on the board.

For practically every game played in the NFL, an over and under number is put up, to be bet on.

Let's assume that the next week, Buffalo is playing New England. Buffalo, is giving up 42 points to the Jets, have been shown to have a porous defense. New England may have a weak offense this year, but Buffalo is weak also offensively.

The oddsmakers take this into consideration as well as the previous points scored for and against both teams, and they also factor in the weather conditions. The game will either be played near Buffalo, New York or Foxboro, Massachusetts, in the cold Northeast. Let's assume the game is played in late November, and there is a possibility of snow. Snowy and frozen conditions inhibit scoring. There are fumbles and slips, of course, but also dropped passes and unexpected falls.

Taking all this into considerations, the oddsmakers come up with a number for the over and under bettors -36.

HOW TO WIN AT SPORTS BETTING

If you bet **over** you're betting that the combined teams' scores adds up to over 36, that is, 37 or more. If you bet **under** you're betting that the combined score is 35 or less. If it comes out at 36, it's a push, and no one wins or loses.

These bets are made at 11-10, allowing the bookies to keep their 4.54% vig, and the gambler must win more than 52.38% of the time in order to beat the bookie.

Some bettors have a flair for this kind of over and under bet, and stick to it exclusively. They've factored in all the elements and maybe get an edge from knowing weather patterns and long term weather forecasts. If there's a blizzard in Buffalo where the game is going to be played and the number is still 36, they're betting under. If it calls for a crisp sunny day, they may go over or may stay away from the action as having no particular edge for them.

In betting over and under games it s easy enough for you to add up all the previous scores and come up with a number, and then to think about weather conditions and subtract from that number if the weather is going to be a negative factor.

There's something else that should be examined in over and under betting - whether or not it is a key game for the teams involved, or for one team.

Generally, important games are lower scoring than unimportant games. Or the game may be important to one team, which may sit on the ball if it has the lead, and play cautiously and safely. The other team may play recklessly and go for the quick points. It's a complex situation that can't be easily answered, but for a clever bettor who thinks about all the factors clearly, it may be a strawberry patch of profits.

Numbers change in over and under betting as they do in the regular pointspread. Money may come in under or over and then the number must be altered. The bookie doesn't want to be "sided" in any situation. Or the weather may change causing the number to either drop or rise. A storm may pass and the number goes down.

The bettor should be some kind of amateur weatherman,or better still, have access to weather reports that are accurate and up-to-date in betting on games. This is true of area with changeable weather, such as the Midwest and the East, particularly the Northeast. In the

Far West, particular in California, weather won't be a factor at all for the most part. And of course, with domed stadiums the weather has been take out of the picture. In games played in domes, everything but weather should be factored in, including the fact that passes will be truer without wind to hinder them. This means fewer interceptions, and depending on the teams, stronger offenses and weaker defenses.

TEASERS

A "teaser" bet is just that. The bookmaker *teases* the gambler into betting on two or more games rather than a single game. Thus the player is "parlaying" his bet; depending on a win in all the games he has wagered on in order to win his single bet.

The general practice in football betting when **parlays,** or more than one game is bet at a single time, is to punish the bettor by not giving him the correct odds.

For example, the chances of picking a winner of just one game is 50% exactly - one chance in two. Of course we've seen that this is not enough to beat the bookie, who gets that 4.54% vigorish or edge.

The chances of picking two games correctly at one time moves to 3-1, or one chance in four. This is so because if we multiply 50% by 50%, we get 25%. It would look like this: 1/2 x 1/2 = 1/4.

However, the teaser bet is not quite simply a sucker bet, because the gambler doesn't just bet on two teams. For example, he is given an inducement by having the bet teased, that is giving him extra points on the games he selects.

The usual situation is this - if the tease is for two games, the bettor is given an extra 6 points and he can make his bet at even-money. If the tease is for 6 1/2 points, then the bettor must lay 11-10, and finally, if the tease is for 7 points, he must give the bookie 6-5 when placing the bet. In order to win, it must always be kept in mind that both games must come out right for the gambler. If he wins one and loses the other, he's down the drain, and loses his bet.

The easiest way to show how a tease wager works is to assume that on one particular Sunday there are two "pick'em" games, that is, games in which neither team is favored over the other. This doesn't happen that often, but it can easily illustrate the fundamentals of the tease bet.

Let's look at a line one theoretical Sunday and notice the following:

SAN DIEGO - Philadelphia Pick

New Orleans - ATLANTA Pick

For the sake of argument, let's say that we have definite feelings about these games. We feel that the home team can win each of these games, but they may be very close, with not more than a field goal separating the teams, when the final score is put up. So, we decide to tease both games.

The bookmaker takes our tease bet, and gives us both San Diego and the Atlanta Falcons as underdogs, each by 6 points. Now, as far as we're concerned, the official line would read as follows:

SAN DIEGO - Philadelphia +6

ATLANTA - New Orleans +6

Instead of a pick'em situation, we have received 6 points for each contest, and instead of laying 11-10, we've made an even-money bet. But we need two wins. If San Diego covers the points, and Atlanta loses by more than 6 points, we've lost the whole wager.

Is a tease in this situation a good bet? We've examined potential tease scores for a number of years, as have other handicappers, and with 6 points added to the line in your favor, the chances of winning a single game move from 50% to roughly 70%. If we could just tease one game, we'd be in clover, but we're forced to tease two games, at least.

We know, from the previous example that to determine the correct odds, we simply multiply the chances of winning one wager by itself to see what the correct odds are for winning two at a time. We saw previously that multiplying 50% by 50%, we got 25%, which are the chances of winning two games at one time without a tease.

So now we multiply 70% by 70% and come up with 49%. How does this compare with an ordinary bet on one game at 11-10? At 11-10, we're giving the bookmaker a 4.54% edge on the bet. At 49%, the bookmaker has a 2% edge (51-49).

If we go further and take 6 1/2 points and have to lay 11-10, or points and we lay 6-5, then the bookmaker is increasing his edge well over his theoretical 4.54% on a single bet.

It seems that our best bet when playing teasers is to stick with the 6 point tease at even-money. However, we must realize that most football betting is illegal, and bookies all over the country may have their own rules. If they require 11-10 when getting a 6 point tease, you don't want to make the bet. You're getting much the worst of it.

Bookmakers will allow teasers on three games as well as two games, but they won't pay you the correct odds for a simple reason. To pick three ordinary games without a tease means that you're bucking 7-1 odds. At 70% x 70% x 70% we will win only 34.3% of the time and we won't be getting correct odds for this. Avoid anything but a two-team teaser.

Most players and bookmakers think of a tease as a true sucker's bet. I've met gamblers who sneer at the teaser bet, but few truly understand it. If you're right on the money with your handicapping, getting those extra six points can be a terrific cushion. And remember, our example was pick'em games. If your team is an underdog by 7 points and how you extend it to +13, that's an awfully thick and big cushion in the NFL.

Look for your spots in the official line each week and if you see situations where teaser bets will make money for you, you can make those 6 point teasers at even money. But do it only to make money; don't do it for the thrill of a gamble.

Remember, your whole purpose in betting on NFL games is to win money...never lose track of that goal.

PARLAYS

It seems natural to move from teasers to parlays, which do not tease points, but make so-called big payoffs to entice gamblers. These are truly sucker bets and we'll show you why.

If we look at the illustrated parlay card on the next page, we see that they offer various payoffs for selections. If we win three out of three, we get 6 for 1. The correct odds are 7-1 when selecting three games.

Remember our old formula - 50% x 50% x 50% or 1/2 x 1/2 x 1/2. Instead of paying off 7-1 or even 6-1, which would be terrible enough, they're paying off *6 for 1*, which comes to only 5-1!

Six for one means this - you get five to one plus your bet back. It's the old sucker way of screwing gamblers.

To show how bad this "for one" is, suppose on an even-money bet, instead of getting 1-1, you received 1 for 1. If you won the bet, all you'd get back was your original dollar and nothing else. You could only lose and never win. It's no different than "heads I win, tails you lose."

When we get up to 5 for 5 as shown on the cards, they're offering 20 for 1, or 19-1, when the correct odds 31-1 or one chance in 32. It's probably more fun to flush your money down the toilet than to make these sucker bets.

The chances of picking 10 out of 10 are an astronomical 1,023-1, which is familiar to roulette and systems players who go broke by quoting this number and telling their listeners that it's a sure thing to double up after every bet, because, after all it's 1,023-1 against losing 10 in a row.

And what do the parlay card sellers pay you for winning 10 out of 10; a measly 175-1. Come on, fellows, give us a break!

Don't even think of betting on parlay cards. Save your money. Either you're going to be a smart bettor or a sucker. If you're a sucker, you're going to lose money and be scorned and laughed at by the bookies.

If you're smart you'll be beating their brains out where it hurts the most, in their pocketbook and nobody will be laughing at you. You'll be treated with respect.

Winners get respect; loser slink out the door. It's your choice.

GETTING INFORMATION

When you decide to take a serious interest in sports betting and decide also that your goal is one thing and one thing only, to make money, then you should absorb all the information you can about the personnel and teams in the NFL. Information and knowledge are powerful tools to use.

The best way to sense a team's strengths and weaknesses is to watch it in action.

For example, you can read all you want about the local teams' quarterback. Probably, if you live in the same town and read the hometown newspapers about your team, you will find that he gets mixed reviews. He'll be the misunderstood darling of one columnist and another one will spend all his time tearing him apart.

The same will hold true for television sports reporters. On Channel 4 they'll love him and on Channel 7 they'll feature all his mistakes. But these are opinions coming to you second-hand, and as far as you're concerned, second-rate. In order to appraise that quarterback you should watch him play.

This doesn't mean that you have to go to the stadium at great expense because unless you have a terrific seat you're going to miss most of the action, and you can't sit on the 30 yard line and get a close-up of that quarterback in action.

Your best chance to see how well he operates is to watch the game on television. Your local station will probably broadcast a number of the games away from home, and even some at home if they're sellouts, and you'll be able to see the team in action on a national or Monday night broadcast occasionally as well.

With instant replay, with reverse angle shots and all the other technical achievements of television, you can leisurely see just how good or how bad he is. He can't hide from the closeness of the TV camera, and all offensive plays begin with the quarterback getting the ball from center, and that's where the camera focuses in.

The quarterback is the key player on any team, but there are other factors and players and positions we're going to deal with that are important, and you should check them out as well. How strong is the defense? What about the nose tackle, the linebackers and the defensive ends? How good is the pass defense? How quick are the cornerbacks in man to man coverage?

The game of football is complex as played by top pros and you have to see them in action to correctly appraise them. You don't have to be a fan, glued to the TV set, but if your serious hard-earned money is being bet, then you should watch and get information to make those crucial judgments. You've got to do better than throw the darts at the board and pick 50% winners.

And if you are not rooting for the home team, you're at a singular and distinct advantage, because you can bet against the team and get that extra point or two in you hometown. And you can get a full picture of how that team is doing, how its strengths and weaknesses are reflected in the scores. There will be enormous coverage in your town. Take advantage of it.

It might be advantageous to read magazines such as *Sports Illustrated*, or subscribe to a weekly like the *Pro Football Weekly*, out of Chicago. Even during football season *Sports Illustrated* doesn't concentrate solely on football, but they dig deep with personalities of the game, and you might get some insights that will help you. Anything that will give you a better feel for the game is important to you.

You want to think of yourself as a professional, not an amateur. The amateurs talk about their team and are either disappointed or elated. You aren't involved in that - you care how the team does only in the sense that it enhances your pocketbook. If your home team was bombed the week before, but you had a big bet on the opponent, then you're elated correctly. Loyalty to professional football teams by fans is often a stale joke, because how loyal are the owners and players to the fans.

Another recommended publication is *The Gold Sheet*, published out of Sunset Boulevard in Los Angeles. It offers a load of information. In the *Pro Football Weekly* and the *Gold Shee*t, you're going to find picks of the weekly games as well as complete analysis of the matchups. Don't blindly follow them. Make your own mind up, but study them. There can always be something you can learn.

During football season there will be a number of "Tout Sheets" which, depending on their arrogance, will assure the subscriber of big win, sometimes up to 70% of the time. That's a remarkable percentage of wins, since, as we'll see, if you could win about 58-60% of the time, you'd retire comfortably, to live a life of luxury.

If these tout sheets can guarantee those kinds of wins, I wonder why they exist at all, since it would pay for the writers to simply bet big bucks and clean up by themselves. Why are they sharing the wealth? Are they altruistic? I doubt it.

What they want is subscribers' money. That's how they make their living. They can't make it by betting, otherwise they'd do that. Why advertise and grind out all that copy when all they have to do is go to the local bookie, or better yet, buy a condo or house in Vegas and just rake in the money? Sounds logical, doesn't it? But somehow they attract suckers who fall for their line.

Some of the tout sheets come up with the favorite word in their vocabulary, week after week. That word is "lock", which is defined as roughly the equivalent of a sure thing. A can't miss situation. But then, why give it away? And some of these locks are not just for the week, they're for the year and some for the decade.

I'm waiting to read about the lock for all time, to eternity. Maybe it's already been advertised and I missed it.

B. The NFL Game - Analysis

The game of football as played in the NFL is much different than football played in colleges. It has to be looked at in an entirely different light. For one thing, the players are more skillful and bigger and stronger and better. The best of the college players moves up to the pros, and even some of the best can't make the grade. NFL football is a brutal sport, played by hard hitting men of exceptional physical strength and stamina. Some positions call for brute strength; others for quickness and still others for intelligence combined with quickness or strength. The NFL is not a league for weaklings and losers. They can't last there.

Although betting on NFL games is involved with numbers, the numbers correlating to the touchdowns, field goals and safeties that add points to a team's score, the game on the field is played by men. We've mentioned this before and will mention it again. It's important.

Sometimes motivation and psychological factors will outweigh brute strength and quickness. Often they'll be the final determinant in who wins and who loses. All of these factors must be taken into consideration and carefully weighed.

Another factor that the public disregards time and time again is consistency. An ironic statement could be made that the betting public consistently disregards consistency. By consistency I mean the general talent and motivation of a team. That doesn't change over a season unless there are crippling injuries to key players. But the injury factor aside, a good team stays good and a weak team stays weak.

In any particular game, a strong team may be upset by a weaker team. It happens a number of times in the course of any season. There are many reasons for this. Sheer bad luck, a bad call by the officials or any number of other factors may lend a hand in these upsets.

And what happens is that the general betting public disregards the overall strength or weakness of the teams and focuses on that game. The oddsmakers understand this principle well and alter the line to take advantage of the misconceptions of the betting public and their overall delusions.

When this happens, a trap situation exists. Let's assume that the Dallas Cowboys have a rather weak team in the process of rebuilding, yet they go and upset a supposedly stronger Washington Redskin team. The next week, Dallas is playing the Giants, but because of their previous showing, instead of being 10 point underdogs to the New York team, they're listed as +3. And they end up getting destroyed by the Giants. The betting public was trapped into thinking that the previous week's upset was how the team really stacked up in strength.

Meanwhile, the Redskins, who were upset by Dallas, are playing a weak Atlanta team. Let's assume theoretically that the Redskins should be at least 10 point favorites against the Falcons, but based on their miserable showing the week before, they're listed as -6. Another trap situation for those betting against the Washington club.

Think in terms of overall consistency. Give each team a rating of relative strength. These ratings may change - you could have been wrong, or there might be injuries or drug problems or whatever, and so you keep the situation fluid. But otherwise, don't get trapped by an outlandish performance on any particular weekend.

The opposite to the above situation holds true as well. Suppose that a strong NFL team had a dismal game the previous Sunday, but now is quoted in the official line in its usual favorite's position, without being penalized in the spread.

Don't be afraid to bet on it, if you feel that it can cover the spread. For example, suppose that the San Francisco 49ers lost the previous week to a weaker team, but now they're playing the Saints and are installed as 7 point favorites. If you feel that the 49ers should easily cover the spread, don't worry about the previous week's performance. Go with the strength and bet them.

If the game had national exposure and a strong team looked horrible, you can be sure that the oddsmaker will set up a situation to fool the betting public. He doesn't really have to go out of his way to do this, because the betting public will fool itself. It will believe that the performance they've seen is indicative of the future, which isn't the case.

In these situations, where the line is sometimes drastically altered to cater to the delusion of the betting public, you'll find some beautiful soft spots to make some real money.

1. MOTIVATIONAL AND LEADERSHIP

Of all the factors that the NFL game deals with, other than talent, there is no greater power than *motivation* . Motivation can be roughly be defined as something that causes a player to act, to do something. It's often an emotional incentive to excel in a particular game.

When a whole team is so motivated, watch out! That team is going to win and win big. That team is going to play over their heads. That team will, in vernacular terms, *kick ass.*

Like most emotions, motivation is not necessarily logical. All kind of things can set it off.

An opposing player's bragging, for instance, has often been known to lift a team to heights previously unknown. You've all heard of examples where a coach will tape this stupid bragging statement on his bulletin board so that it rubs into the psyche of all his players. Especially if the bragging also contains a contemptuous statement as to the opponents' abilities. Sometimes, a person at one position knocks his opposite number, telling the press that the man he's covering or facing is weak, untalented or whatever.

When an NFL player does this, he's knocking a pro at the game, a man who makes his living playing football. The player so attacked may feel that the braggart is trying to take the bread off his table, trying not only to hurt his ego, but hurt his family, by lowering the estimation his owners will have about him at the next contract talks. Then watch out! The braggart is going to be punished. The player attacked will be thinking..."that fool says I'm just a jerk-off and a has-been. Well, I'm going to show him this Sunday. I'm gonna make him wish he never opened his mouth. I'm gonna hurt him. I'm gonna..." and you can fill in the rest.

The one thing is, you don't want to be the guy this player is gunning for.

Coaches and Motivation

Coaches have a great deal to do with motivation. That's one of the key elements of their job, to motivate their players to go out and win. Some coaches knock their players and in this way they think they'll get them up to top performance. Others praise the players and feel that that will help their performance. Some coaches are strict disciplinarians and others are very loose. Generally, a passive coach will get poor results.

Whether a coach is strict or not, if he is involved with his players, his players will do better. There are exceptions to all statements. Bill Walsh was a very successful coach with the San Francisco 49ers, but after he left the team, the players groused about his withdrawn personality.

A strict disciplinarian like Vince Lombardi got the most out of his players by fear. They were out there a few weeks after having broken legs, running wind sprints, afraid that Lombardi would consider them pussies. When Lombardi called a meeting for 8 in the morning, they were there at 7:30 or the doors would be slammed shut and they'd come in with their heads hung low.

There is no single way to motivate a team, because that team is made up of many individuals, and each individual has to be treated as a separate person. An interior lineman may have to be badgered to stay in shape, while a cornerback may take pride in his physical condition. A quarterback may have to be pampered; a kicker may just have to be left alone.

But you must be aware of the coaches and their abilities as far as motivation is concerned. Those who are great motivators, who get their teams up for the big games are coaches to follow. Bet against those that are passive, who make excuses blaming their teams for losses. These are whiners and losers.

Don't bet on complainers.

MONEY AND MOTIVATION

Football has become a big money industry, and after a long stretch of being kept out of the money, the players got wise and demanded their rightful share. After much infighting, they've been getting big bucks also. They're getting their share of the pie. Million dollar contracts for key players and first round draft picks are commonplace.

How does the big money affect the motivation of players.?

It depends. Again, we have no one clear cut answer, and if a bettor is looking for the simple key to winning at football, then he'll end up in the clutches of a tout because he doesn't want to think for himself. We've got to look at each situation separately and carefully. But we can make money if we figure them out.

For example, a team gives up two key players and a high draft pick to get a hotshot college quarterback, whom the general manager or the coach describes as a "quality player, able to fit right into our scheme of things. He's an NFL player right now."

So far, the scheme of things at this team has been steady losses, so the new guy will fit right in. Already, the team has mortgaged the future to get him, and if they've given up a linebacker and cornerback for example, then this new quarterback will be playing catch-up ball all season long as their opponents score almost at will.

It is extremely rare for a college quarterback, no matter of what quality, to step into the NFL and be just as good as he was in college. By just as good, we means as dominant.

He's not facing the East Carolina defensive line, averaging 190 pounds, while he's guarded by a line that averages 260 pounds. No, now he's facing NFL defensive linemen who would just as soon eat him up for lunch and spit out his bones and sleep like babies that night.

He's facing pass rushers who are 275 pounds of muscle, who can cripple him if they really want to, who can snap his back as if it was made of matchsticks. A new element has entered his life. Fear!

He no longer has a safe pocket, as he did in college, where he can leisurely get rid of the ball because he's protected. No, now he must have a "quick release", because if he doesn't, the hot breath of some sadistic defensive end will first burn a hole in his skin, and then he'll feel the sickening power of a blindside hit that will knock the breath and eventually the spirit out of him.

There is only so much punishment a young quarterback can take before he becomes gun shy and just throws the ball away or eats it. If he throws prematurely, there will be a lot of interceptions, and soon he'll be pushed out again to the field to take more punishment.

This horrible scenario is repeated over and over again, season after season. Be aware of it. No matter what the hype is, and believe me there will be hype - bet against these young untried quarterbacks. If a team is smart, if a coach knows what he's doing, he'll save the quarterback and put him in sparingly for a season or two, "seasoning him." And he'll build a defensive line that will protect him.

But the coach is often under pressure himself. He's gotten his star college quarterback to replace the ancient relic now playing for the team, and the crowds will be screaming for the hotshot as his team keeps losing. He'll get pressure from the press and from the owners, who don't get their bones broken cashing their checks week after week. And so, he'll relent. When he does, step in and bet against that quarterback and his million dollar contract. Start yourself off on your own million dollars.

Other positions are different, because there isn't that much pressure. A solid linebacker in college who's a first round draft choice can fit right into a lineup. Many have done so their first season. They don't stand out as quarterbacks do. When a quarterback makes a mistake, everyone is aware of it. When a linebacker makes a mistake, only the coaches and a couple of players may realize this.

He won't have that constant pressure, and he's part of a group of linebackers.

Any lineman is in the same boat. He may get beaten and beaten up in the line, but he's learning, and his spot isn't a key to success. The team can afford to let him make mistakes and learn his position thoroughly.

However, with cornerbacks, we have a situation almost analogous to the quarterback. When a cornerback makes a mistake, it's often a dilly, and the whole world is aware of it. If he misses coverage, and a long gain or TD comes as a result, there he is in the open, hanging his head. He can't hide anyplace.

The hotshot cornerbacks and safeties in college have not been up against the speed and savvy of NFL ends. They'll generally be eaten alive their first season, no matter how many zeros are on their contract, and experienced and veteran quarterbacks will take advantage of them.

In the NFL, where performance translates into contract dollars, no one feels sorry for anyone else. If a linebacker is limping, you can be sure that blocking back will be trying to cut his legs off. If a cornerback doesn't properly know how to cover a star receiver, you can be sure he'll be tested over and over again, till he's staggering around the backfield panting and gasping and flushed with defeat.

So far we've discussed newcomers. What about the veterans who get big contracts? As a rule, they won't be complacent because of the big money. They have pride, otherwise they couldn't have lasted in one of the most brutal sports ever invented by man, NFL football.

It's a sport where injuries are commonplace, where it is rare for any athlete, no matter what his position, to go through a career without some kind of crippling injury or serious operation. And some players have annual operations on shoulders, feet and worst of all, on their knees. If you've ever come across a former NFL player watch how he walks. A great star like Joe Namath will spend the rest of his life in pain because of bad knees. Men who still play the game can't dress themselves or walk down stairs without aid. The game takes its toll.

From my observations over the years, I feel that big contracts to

HOW TO WIN AT SPORTS BETTING

veterans won't change their pride or their ability to play the game well. If a veteran has been traded to a contender and is given a big contract to fill a niche or weakness in that club, he will try and do the best he can, maybe even play over his head, particularly if he's come from a losing team. He can now smell the possibility of a Super Bowl ring, and that's a great motivation for an NFL player. It's beyond money; it's now in the realm of enduring pride.

A veteran who has only one or two seasons left and is traded to a mediocre team may tell a different story. He's taken a lot of punishment, and he may want to preserve his body as best he can. He's not a young star anymore and he's gotten wise with the passing years. He's not throwing out his body in abandon, taking whatever pain and punishment will be meted out. He'll be careful, and being careful in the NFL relates to mediocrity. Watch these situations.

THE REVENGE FACTOR

Teams have long memories; sometimes lasting more than one season. For example, a team humiliated by another team a season before may build up its strength to turn the tables on that team.

What often happens is that during one season, early on, Team A crushes Team B. When this happens, and they meet again later the season, the general betting public looks at that earlier game and says, "hey, Team A is only -10 over Team B and they've already beaten them, 35-7. This is a sure bet on Team A." And then they're surprised when Team B upsets Team A straight-up. This situation happens over and over again in the NFL. Just look at the records of previous years to verify this.

OWNERSHIP

Not all football results come from the playing personnel. Often these same results have come from decisions made off the field by the owners of the ballclubs. Strong involved ownership means winning teams. Weak or stingy ownership means losing teams. In many cases, it's as simple as that.

Or we get a case where the owners, who have made money in some other enterprise, meddle in football decisions that they know nothing about, always to the detriment of the team.

Even astute owners can make big mistakes. A good example is Al Davis, who has been so busy deciding where to play his Raiders, whether in Irwindale, Los Angeles, Oakland or elsewhere that the team, once one of the premier clubs in the NFL with the best overall won-lost record, has become one of the mediocre teams. He's done an outstanding job in court, winning millions of dollars in damages from other NFL teams, but he's not had much of a success on the gridiron.

Draft picks have turned out poorly, trades haven't panned out, and although he has one of the biggest bankrolls at his disposal and pay his team very well, there isn't much of the old spirit on the Raiders, a spirit that characterized the team in the previous year.

Contrast the Raiders with the San Francisco '49ers, where the owner Edward De Bartolo, Jr. wisely left the football decisions to people like Bill Walsh, who was a genius at getting the proper draft picks to help his team. With the owner's millions behind him, he traded for the best players and paid them well.An example is the $1.1 million paid to their backup quarterback, Steve Young, when the average backup quarterback was paid about $350,000.

When you combine an open pocketbook by the owners with the astute football knowledge of a general manager and coach, you've got a winner. This was no more evident than during the long dynasty of the Dallas Cowboys, who combined Tex Schramm's and Tom Landry's football knowledge with an open pocketbook, and produced winner after winner. No matter what seemed to happen to other clubs, the Cowboys were in the playoffs year after year. They were consistent, because whatever weaknesses they had were plugged up by the owners and coaches. And their team was stocked deep with talent.

They were way ahead of their time in scouting by computer, carefully weighing all the possible players in the draft, when other clubs were groping their way in the same manner used in the by-gone days of pro football.

The Rams have the same situation. They have an owner who isn't afraid to spend money and a coaching staff that knows how to use the talent wisely, and picks talent, such as Jim Everett, a "franchise type" quarterback.

Don Shula at Miami had Joe Robbie behind him with the bucks and Shula, one of the wisest of coaches was able to produce winners year after year. Then, when there were disagreements between the owner and Shula, the club started to disintegrate and lose its winning ways.

Pittsburgh had the same relationship between a fine coach, Chuck Noll and the Rooney family, and they produced some of the finest teams the NFL ever knew, stocked with players like Terry Bradshaw, Lynn Swann, Joe Greene and Franco Harris. One could go on and on about that roster, which completely dominated the NFL when they were all together.

The New York Giants, which at times have fielded brilliant teams, have been hurt by squabbles between the Mara brothers, who own the club. Despite having the tremendous New York area market, this team hasn't done what it could have accomplished because of the weakness of the ownership.

Some places, such as Atlanta and Green Bay have had weak ownership for many years and have suffered as a result. Atlanta has never been a factor in the NFL, and Green Bay, after the glorious years of Vince Lombardi and the Pack, has suffered for many years in mediocrity. They have a situation where the town itself is the owner of the club, and suffer also from the fact that this late in the 20th Century a small town is fielding a big league team. The players, particularly black players have been unhappy for years with their treatment in Green Bay. Some say the situation is changing, that the Pack is Back, but that's been said for a long time now.

Phoenix, which now boasts the Cardinals, is run as a private fiefdom, with fans complaining about escalating prices and lower grade teams.

When you have greedy ownership, which is usually reflected by a team leaving a major market for another city purely on the basis of financial gain, that team is sure to suffer. St. Louis lost to Phoenix and the owner of the Colts, took the team from Baltimore to Indianapolis.

Never mind that the Colts were one of the great franchises in football while in Baltimore. Never mind that it had fielded so many legendary teams led by Johnny Unitas, and was, in some ways responsible for two of the biggest moments in NFL history; the 1958 TV game against the New York Giants which put the NFL indelibly in the public's consciousness, and the 1968 Super Bowl game with Joe Namath and the Jets, which made the league what it is today, and made the Super Bowl the premier attraction in sports in America.

When the almighty buck beckoned, Baltimore was left in the lurch. Only in America! No where else in the world would such tradition be disregarded and teams moved just for the sake of an owner's greed.

When you read about problems in ownership, when owners squabble or talk about moving franchises, then pay attention because you can find good spots for your bets.

Go against the team that is constantly badmouthing its fans and talking of moving. This kind of talk takes the heart out of any incentive for the club to perform well. It loses the home field advantage for the team, because the players dread having to play before the home folks constantly booing them.

Watch these situations closely.

It's great when a home team advantage turns into a detriment and yet the other side is laying points on the advantage. You're getting extra value for your money, always an ideal situation. For example, if Team A, wracked by dissension, with the owner talking about moving the club, is playing at home against team B, and Team A is given its usual 3 points for the home field advantage, go against Team A.

It probably should be penalized 3 points for playing before a half-empty house that is booing the players even during their introduction.

COACHING STAFF

As much as the talent and personnel on the team, the coaches play an important role in determining winners or losers. The head coach sets the tone of the team, and he has the power to play certain players and to bench others. He also determines, either alone or through assistants, the type of offense and defense that the team will use.

Certainly coaches can make a big difference. A coach like Vince Lombardi with his peculiar work ethic and determination that "winning isn't everything, it's the only thing" brought a weak Green Bay franchise to life and made it a dynasty. Then he turned around a complacent Washington Redskin team before his untimely death. Lombardi inspired fear in his players; and in this way he got the best out of his personnel. He also had a multitude of fine players, such as Bart Starr, Paul Hornung and Ray Nitschke.

Coaches who are like Lombardi can be likened to the General Pattons. Americans love the situation. A sloppy and slovenly squad of soldiers is hanging around without proper uniforms and without proper security, and suddenly this big-time general comes in and shakes them up. They're demoted or warned to get on the stick, and as they stand there shivering we all get a charge out of it. I guess this is so because we're thinking "better him than me."

Nobody likes a disciplinarian unless results are shown, which lead to a group of coaches that are strict disciplinarians but don't develop winning teams.

Rather than mentioning actual names in this section, we're just going to deal with various types of coaches. A quick study of the teams your following will easily reveal the type. The disciplinarians may or may not be effective. In the end, Patton was disgraced and a quiet but effective type like General Omar Bradley superseded him both in rank and in the affection of his men and his country.

After all, discipline can go too far, and can border on sadism.

Some NFL coaches, particularly those who may have coached on the college level, think that they have a bunch of kids on the team that need to be kicked in the butt all the time. But these aren't boys, these are men, many of them veterans, mature pros who won't take the same kind of crap from coaches that they did in high school or college, when they were just helpless kids.

The disciplinarian better show good results; there has to be a rationale for his actions, otherwise the team will lose respect for him and not play up to its potential. After all, men like to be praised, not put down all the time. There's time for everything, but if all the coach will give is miserable tongue lashings, then the players may avoid him, sulk and ask to be traded rather than play up to or greater than their God-given talents.

We should take advantage of this kind of coach, by following his team carefully. Are they rebelling? Is there dissension? The opposite of harmony usually forebodes ill. Losses, not wins. When you see this happening on a team, don't wring your hands, but put your hands in your pocket, take out the cold cash and bet against the team.

The opposite of the disciplinarian is the coach who is entirely passive who lets the squad do pretty much what they want to do , reasoning that these are pros and grown men and are paid well and know what the hell they're doing. This works well sometimes, and has worked with a renegade team like the LA Raiders in the past.

The danger however,and it's a big danger that shows up late in the season, that this hands=off approach leads to a poorly conditioned team.

As we know, the NFL brand of football is a brutal business and a poorly conditioned team just can't hold up the whole season. Look at the stats while you're studying the seasonal records, and see if certain teams fall apart in the third and fourth quarters. This can mean that the players are in poor shape.

I've watched games where I've noticed players on one team gulping oxygen while the other team's squad was walking around. I put that down to poor conditioning and I started betting against that team, and it paid off. They'd take early leads and fade out. Games I had thought I lost to the spread came back miraculously to life, and suddenly, in the fourth quarter, my spread was covered.

I was making money betting against teams in poor shape.

By this time, you understand that when I tell you not to be a fan, it pays off in a lot of ways. Your main interest is making money, so you want to look deeper into situations than the average fan. The fan will moan about how his team did a foldo for the third game in a row.

On the other hand, you'll be cashing winning tickets on those games, because you've seen the reason for the poor late showing. You'll be smarter than the average fan and smarter than the bookie. You've looked deeper into what is going on with a particular team and taken advantage of it.

The teams where low-keyed coaches fit in best are teams with a bunch of talent, where players don't have to be nursed along or taught much.

The Dallas Cowboys in their heyday with Tom Landry was a perfect example. Landry was cool on the sidelines, and he never seemed to get ruffled or elated. He was constant, and he was the perfect coach for his team, which had quarterbacks like Roger Staubach, who was a great team leader.

What Landry lent to the squad was innovation and direction and it turned out to be a winning combination. Now that he's gone, Jimmy Johnson is the new coach with a squad of young players, and he is known or has a reputation of a strong disciplinarian. We'll see what happens.

I think patience is better than discipline in these situations but you judge for yourself. Watch the results as the Cowboys attempt to rebuild and see how they do. If the coaching turns out to be at odds with what the team accomplishes, then go against the Cowboys. None of these moves should be made blindly.

There are no simple answers in betting on NFL football. It's a study of complex situations, but we're constantly showing you what to look for and how to take advantage of the various situations presented to you.

But you must study and then you must make the proper moves by putting your bankroll at risk on what you believe.

As we mentioned before, beware of coaches that publicly berate their teams to the media. A good example is Mike Ditka of the Chicago Bears, who was constantly badmouthing his team to the press, and during games was walking around the sidelines throwing things when he was displeased by the play of his personnel.

Compare him to Tom Landry, who remained cool and said what he had to say behind closed doors. It's an easy comparison. With superb personnel Landray built a dynasty that lasted almost two decades, while Ditka had only one Super Bowl winner with the same superb personnel.

Another good thing about Landry was his innovation, such as the flex defense and the shotgun. Look for coaches with imagination. Like all other fields, the coaching in the NFL is mostly mediocre, with a bunch of plodders having no imagination, just trying to hold onto their jobs by courting the goodwill of the owners. They don't get winning results from their players and they are followers, using whatever someone else invented in their offense or defense.

When a plodder faces an innovator, I go with the innovator, especially if its an important game. The innovative coach will have something new up his sleeve, and will know how to counteract every move the plodder makes, because the plodder won't change.

How can you tell which is which? Simply watch games on TV and read as much as you can about other games you haven't watched. Scores don't tell the full story. Study the coaches carefully. Often they'll tell you the true story of whether or not you're going to cash many winning tickets.

Some coaches are inept, and put too many players on the field at one time or have the wrong players there or waste time when precious seconds count. There are a number of them in the NFL, and when the two squads seem evenly matched, go with the coach who is competent.

If both are inept, why torture yourself. Stay away from the game.

PLAYER PERSONNEL

Now we come to the players that make up the team, the heart and soul of NFL football.

In today's game, the offense is one unit and the defense another, and within those units there are specialties. Defensive personnel don't stay in for all four downs. In running situations, certain players come in. In passing situations, other players are used. Still others on special teams are in on fourth down situations.

The same holds true for the offense.

The quarterback will always be anchoring the team, but the running backs and receivers will change from down to down. Tight ends with bulk and muscle will replace quicker but smaller ends in short yardage situations.

The combinations are endless, stopped only by a coach's imagination. Along with the changes, there are coaches covering every conceivable situation; quarterback coaches and interior linemen coaches and so forth.

Let's begin with the offense, and analyze what you're to look for in order to cash in those winning tickets.

2. THE OFFENSE

We're going to divide the offense into several categories. First and foremost, we'll deal with the quarterback. Then the running backs, then the receivers and finally the offensive linemen. Each play a key role in scoring points, and weakness in any one category may very well sabotage the entire offense.

The primary job of the offense is to score points, and when ahead, to try and hold onto the ball as long as possible, using up valuable time, and keeping the pressure on the other team. This is called ball control and it is best carried out by a good running game, or, lacking that, having a quarterback who can throw short passes consistently and accurately.

THE QUARTERBACK

In NFL football, the most important player is the quarterback. He will handle the ball on all offensive plays and he is responsible for the entire offense since everything flows out of his hands. He will either get the ball directly from the center in a quick exchange, with the quarterback's hands between the center's legs or he will have the ball snapped to him in what has been called the **shotgun**, with the quarterback standing several yards back. But the quarterback will get the ball one way or another.

As players throughout the NFL have gotten bigger, so have the quarterbacks. At one time they could be comparatively small men, and heights of 5'9" didn't hurt. Today, with huge linemen rushing, an undersigned quarterback is six feet tall. Teams look for size, and a small quarterback in the NFL these days is 6'2". Preferably, his size should be at least 6'4".

It's been a trend for a while now, and the trend is to taller and bulkier quarterbacks. Some of them are really big and can hold their own against all but the strongest linemen.

There are two basic reasons for this height requirement. First of all, the quarterback must be able to see the field, look for primary and secondary receivers and he won't be able to do this with line-men who are six and a half feet tall rushing him with their hands over their heads. Secondly, in the NFL, a quarterback takes a lot of physical punishment, and he must be able to handle it.

But no matter how big he is, the quarterback must have other qualities. He must, first of all, be able to throw the ball well. He must be able to throw it short with a soft touch, and he must be able to throw the deep bomb.

He doesn't have to throw too deeply, for he will have speedy receivers who can make things happen when they catch the ball, but he has to be able to get that ball out there 40 to 50 yards, necessary. And with short passes, he must have that touch so that the receivers can handle the ball comfortably. It's dangerous to have a hard thrower on short passes, because when that ball bounces off the receiver's hands, it's up for grabs.

John Elway, despite his ability, has always had trouble getting that soft touch on his passes, and he's failed miserably in Super Bowl games.

On the other hand, the greatest master of the short pass, Joe Montana, with his ultra soft touch, has been a constant winner in the Super Bowl. What it boils down to is ball control. Although Elway has sometimes led some extraordinary drives with his team behind and precious seconds to play, Joe Montana is *always* capable of those drives.

A quarterback with a soft touch on his short passes is essential if the running game is lacking. With a good running game, his short passes are an extra weapon that forces the defense to spread itself too thinly over the field.

In addition to the arm, the quarterback must have one important essential, and that's leadership. Leadership comes with time, and with respect by the other players. It also comes with confidence. A Joe Namath was an instant leader. He had the arm and he could move a ball club and his leadership caught on immediately. He had one other thing that seems essential now to an NFL quarterback. He had a quick release.

In the fast game of NFL football, a quick release really helps, because the quarterback has only a couple of seconds to scan the field and throw the ball. He has to get rid of the ball quickly, or he will be sacked.

But let's get back to leadership. Even if a quarterback in the old days didn't have such a great arm, if he had leadership, it was enough. One example, that comes to mind is Billy Kilmer. When Kilmer played for the Redskins, it was almost a joke watching his wobbly passes, but he won games, because he won the respect of his teammates. He was a leader.

As we stated, sometimes leadership takes time, and sometimes it is immediate.

The smart coaches move their quarterbacks along slowly, even though the team is losing. It's the proper thing to do. It seasons the quarterback and gives him the correct feel of the game.

Being an NFL quarterback is a learning process, and the learning never stops. That's because coaches are constantly coming up with new defenses, new ways to get to the quarterback or thwart this game.

We are always watching the quarterback situation for that gives us the best clue as to the strength of the team. If a hotshot quarterback is signed out of college and rushed into a starting position immediately, he's usually worth betting against. If the oddsmakers recognize this as well, and you can't get the correct points, lay off the game.

But if the betting public is entranced with one of these wonders and you can get value for your money, go against the team featuring the new quarterback. The fans want to see him succeed, and so does the betting public, who believe all the hype the media is capable of churning out. You should, however, look at the hard cold facts before making a bet.

Coaches who rush quarterbacks are usually inept and are catering to the owners rather than the team. The owner wants the stands filled, and wants an instant winner. So he pushes to coach to play his new quarterback out of a big time college, the one he just signed to a five year, $10 million contract.

If the coach was competent, he'd tell the owner that he should be patient, that he'll put him in spots during the season, and perhaps start him in a year or two. A coach who can't stand up to an owner loses the confidence of his players. Another reason to go against the team he coaches.

Finally, to be a winner, a quarterback must be able to smell that goal line, to get the team to score that TD. Great quarterbacks lift the team by their own example. They'll put themselves on the line and carry the ball on a bootleg if necessary. The goal line is there and the six points is there, and they'll put those points on the board for you.

The opposite is the quarterback who gets cautious at the goal line, who won't take a chance. Sometimes its the coach's fault as well.

Then there's the quarterback who takes the heart out of his team by throwing an interception when down at the opponent's 3 yard line. When this happens often enough, the coach gets gun shy as well and calls for running plays when in scoring position. So, instead of 7 points the team is content with 3 points, and your bet is down the tubes, because the spread wasn't covered.

This happens at the other end of the field as well. The team takes over at the six-yard line (its own) and runs three plays, all running plays, that moves the ball to the 11 yard line. Than the team kicks and the opposing squad now has beautiful field position on the 40 yard line of the opponents. And they run in some kind of score.

If the coach doesn't have faith in his own quarterback, why should you ?

Avoid betting on teams that can't produce 7 points when they should, and play cautiously deep in its own part of the field. If possible, when the points are right, bet against these teams and these quarterbacks.

But no matter what the situation, the first thing you must do when evaluating personnel on any team is look at the quarterback and make a decision. That's the key to winning bets - knowing the strengths and weaknesses of the men who handle the ball on every offensive play.

RUNNERS

The bread and butter plays in the NFL, those calling for a gain of three to five yards, aren't as flashy as the passes, which sometimes eat up ten times that yardage, but they're necessary for a winning team. To get this kind of steady production, you need a solid runner. A great runner is even better, but often a great runner dominates the game to the detriment of the quarterback, and running alone isn't sufficient to win in the NFL.

In the college game a magnificent runner of the order of Herschel Walker lifted the Georgia Bulldogs to national prominence. Not in the pros. He must be an integral part of the offensive machine to be effective. Alone as a star, he may put on the stats, as O.J. Simpson did at Buffalo, but the team will still have losing seasons.

The answer is in balance.

It was there with Larry Csonka and Bob Griese at Miami. In fact they had runners to spare with the flashy Mercury Morris in the backfield at the same time. Franco Harris and Terry Bradshaw certainly made for a magnificent balanced attack that was one of the reason for the Steelers' great success during their wonderful years.

What the runner does primarily is take the pressure off the quarterback. Without a running game, the defense can key in on the quarterback play after play, rushing him, covering the receivers and making life generally miserable for the passing game. With a quality runner in the backfield, the situation changes. Now the defense is miserable, with just too many options to cover.

This is particularly true if the runner can give the team first down yardage of at least 4 yards. The quarterback is at ease. He doesn't have to pass on second down. He has that option. The defense is scattered and not only has to defend against the possibility of a pass, but also against the run.

To gain this type of yardage, the runner doesn't have to be brilliant. He can just be a bruiser who can put those yards on the board. Riggins of the Redskins was just such a player. Big and powerful he was always a threat inside, but if the defense tightened against the short yardage run, he could bowl over the linemen and go all the way, as he did on one memorable Super Bowl play.

Sometimes it's better to have the bruising kind of quarterback who simply grinds out the yards. He's not a star and he doesn't expect to be treated like a star. He gets the yards in short yardage situations, and he's willing to block On the other hand, some of the great runners in NFL history ended up as primadonnas who ran the ball and left the blocking to others.

Another good attribute the bruising runner can have is as a pass catcher. It is usually in short yardage situations, going for the first down. He'll be surrounded by monster linebackers and will be taking his lumps, but he'll put his body on the line in these situations, again, something primadonnas aren't expected to do.

If I studied two teams matched against each other, I'd always pick the balanced attack, with a solid, even pedestrian running back in balance with a strong quarterback.

That certainly seems to be the best combination for winning. When the quarterback, such as Elway of the Broncos, has the brunt of the offensive attack riding on his arm, he can have success, but eventually, he can't do it by himself, not in the big games. Good coaches should be able to take advantage of unbalanced attacks. There's only so much an arm can do, but the legs of a determined runner, churning up the yardage, can hurt the defense in a lot of ways.

It may be fun to read the stats on superb runners like Eric Dickerson, but give me the bread and butter guy any day. I remember watching a few TV games when Herschel Walker was performing for the Dallas Cowboys. The commentators were oohing and aahing over his strength and his moves, but Dallas kept losing the games, and weren't covering the spreads.

So remember, balance in the offensive attack. Look for it. It will pay off your bills as you cash in the winning tickets.

THE OFFENSIVE LINE

So far we've concentrated on the individual stars, the quarterbacks and running backs, the guys who are always in the limelight. On any NFL team, the exact opposite of stars, of players in the public's eye, are the men who make up the offensive line. All they can do is get down in the trenches and block and take punishment and come up muddy and hurt and do their thing over and over again. They can't make tackles, they can't do anything that awards them applause from the thousands that watch the game.

And worse, they'll be called for penalties, holding penalties that will really hurt their team at crucial times. I've heard the fans screaming at the center or guard or tackle on the offensive line after these holding calls, especially if the penalty nullifies a terrific gain. And of course, watching on TV, the camera focuses in on the guilty individual who hangs his head a bit as he goes back to the huddle.

But these men are in every play blocking out monster linebackers, defensive tackles and ends, nose tackles, players of extraordinary skill and speed, and above all, strength. They've got to stop them some way.

Probably there's holding on every play in the NFL. The secret is in how to avoid getting the whistle blown by the line judge. So, these unsung heroes are the topic of this section.

If a team doesn't have a strong offensive line, then all the flashy quarterbacks and runners in the world aren't going to help them.

The offensive linemen, unlike other players, aren't that specialized. They have to be able to accomplish two basic things and to accomplish them well.

First of all, they must stop the defense on passing plays, holding their ground and preventing anyone from getting to the quarterback. They protect the pocket. If the line is porous, and the defense breaks through, then the quarterback is going to be sacked or hurried. In either situation, disaster usually follows in the way of a fumble, big lost yardage or an interception.

Some coaches build their offensive line to protect the quarterback. That is their basic reason for being. However, in those situations, we have an unbalanced attack with the emphasis on passing.

With a balanced attack, which, as we have seen, is much more preferable, the linemen must do other yeoman duty. They must have the strength to surge forward and knock out the defensive line and the linebackers, so that the running game comes alive.

If they can't do both of these things, defend the quarterback against the pass rush, and have that surge to open up spots for the runners, then the line is going to be a liability to the team. You're going to see a club that has trouble moving the ball and putting points up on the scoreboard.

Winning NFL teams have as their mainstay the strong offensive line. Teams that can pour in the points have those granite blocks up there defending the quarterback and smashing apart the opposing line when its a running play. You must examine the offensive line if you're a serious bettor. Watch how they do when you have the TV set on. Unless you see the line in action, you can't know much. There are no stats on interior line blocks. Or knocking down linebackers.

The running game stats and the passing yardage will also tell you a lot, but there's nothing like watching the game itself. Instead of concentrating on the passer or runner, as 99% of the fans do, keep your eyes on the offensive line. See how well they perform. This will give you a clue to the overall strength of the team, especially early in the season, before you have yardage stats to fall back on.

Sometimes a team comes alive and the scores mount up just because a couple of weaknesses in the offensive line have been shored up. This kind of information is looked for by the pros at betting, not by the amateurs or the fans. A runner may increase his average per run, or a quarterback may suddenly be moving his team up and down the field. They may not have changed a bit in talent. What's happened is that the offensive line has been strengthened.

Read about trades and draft picks. See what positions are dealt for, and see if interior linemen have been replaced on a mediocre team. That may be the key to an emerging team, a so-so team that suddenly wins games and covers spreads. Very few people look at these factors, but you should. That's keeping way ahead of the oddsmakers and bookies, especially early in the season.

Conversely, don't lay points or give away points when betting on a team with poor offensive linemen. You're going to take an awful chance, and generally an awful beating, doing this.

One final note: If you study the behavior of offensive linemen carefully, you will learn a great deal. If there are a lot of holding penalties called against the linemen, then they may not be strong enough to hold back the defense, or they may be protecting a quarterback who's injured. When I see a strong center getting called for holding a few times in a game, then I immediately think of his quarterback. Is he under orders to stop the nose tackle at all costs to protect an injured quarterback? That's often a clue to an injury that the team doesn't want to make public.

THE RECEIVING GAME

Since NFL football is the darling of the media, particularly television, the game has been changed time and time again to feature offensive action, for that's what the fans like. They want to see touchdowns scored, they want spectacular plays.

They're not interested in battles in the trenches between 290 pound linemen grunting and pushing each other around. They want to see a kickoff returned for a touchdown, not the ball downed in the end zone. That's why NFL teams now kick off from the 35 yard line instead of the 40.

And one of the most exciting plays in football is the long gainer, when a quarterback steps into the pocket, pumps his arm a couple of times and lets loose with a tremendous pass to a receiver thirty or forty yards down the field. That's real action, something the fans can relate to. That's why there's a rule that a defensive player can only bump a receiver once within 5 yards of the line of scrimmage. Before that rule, wide receivers were often stymied, and the emphasis was on passes to the bigger, tight ends, not to the lithe and speedy wide receivers.

At one time, it was a strictly man-to-man battle between cornerbacks and safeties and the receivers. Today the game has changed drastically. There now are zone defenses, with the cornerbacks given specific areas to cover, and as the receiver moves out of one zone, he finds himself covered in another zone. The zone negates the big passing play, and who knows, maybe in the future it will be outlawed in the same way that zone defenses are outlawed in the NBA.

The ideal offense is to have a superb passer combine with two great receivers. One receiver can generally be covered by the defense, but two receivers of equal ability are too much of a burden for all but the premier pass defenses.

Examples were John Stallworth and Lyn Swann of Pittsburgh, combined with the passing arm of Terry Bradshaw. Mark Duper and Mark Clayton combined with Dan Marino at one point to provide an awesome situation that won a lot of games and piled on the points. That's what you need if you're betting on a team, points, especially if you're giving away points by wagering on the favorite. Let's worry about the defense later. Right now we need points. And an inspired passing game with fleet footed receivers is the easiest way to get those points.

Even one receiver, if he is of the caliber of Jerry Rice of the San Francisco '49ers, can make a difference, if he has a coach and a quarterback that takes advantage of his skills. With a Joe Montana able to throw very accurate short passes to other receivers, Jerry Rice eventually gets loose for the big play.

When a receiver is injured, whether he is a star by himself or in tandem with another receiving star, then you must examine the situation carefully. Without a premier receiver, it's a difficult task to get those points on the board, and you have to be very careful about laying points when that happens.

When a team suffers in any of the offensive categories that we've mentioned so far, the pass, the run, the receivers, the offensive line, then the burden to win often shifts to the defense. And that's what we're going to examine now, the other aspect of winning football, the defensive team.

3. The Defensive Team

As defenses became more sophisticated, defensive stars emerged, often as brilliant as the offensive prima donnas. There was Dick Butkus of the Bears, there's Lawrence Taylor of the New York Giants, just to mention a couple of extraordinary linebackers, a position not known in the early days of NFL football, when seven men lined up on the offensive line and seven on the defensive line and they slugged it out for yardage, the game resembling a rugby match in the mud.

Without a Ronnie Lott patrolling the deep part of his defensive backfield, the '49ers certainly wouldn't have had the success they enjoyed during the 1980s. If you don't have a strong defense, then you're going to give up a lot of points.

You're going to put a ton of pressure on the offensive team, and you're going to strangle them in a come-from-behind game time and time again. And if the defense is on the field too long, it gets fatigued and weary, and starts to fall apart late in the game and late in the season. As Vince Lombardi stated "fatigue makes cowards of us all." He knew what he was talking about.

On the other hand, with a strong defensive team, you take pressure off the offense. You allow them to concentrate on what they do best, score points. They don't have to play catch up football. The defense gives them good field position, often cuts the field in half for them.

It's one thing to have to go 90 yards for a touchdown; it's another to go only 40 yards. A solid defense creates excellent field position time and time again.

But that's not all it does. It creates turnovers, giving the ball back to its own team. It forces the other team's defense to stay on the field an inordinate amount of time, tiring and fatiguing the other squad. It can also put points on the board, which are unexpected blessings, by recovering fumbles and running them in for touchdowns or making interceptions and galloping them in for the score.

In other words, a strong defense can do a lot of things to win games for the team.

Astute coaches hire great defensive coaches and give them a certain amount of freedom. Even a stubborn man like Mike Ditka had a Buddy Ryan working for him. Ryan was an innovative and brilliant defensive coach, and he was immediately hired on as a head coach by the Philadelphia Eagles.

A coach that doesn't pay attention to his defense, but concentrates on his offense, is sapping the strength of his team as much as if he traded away his star quarterback. One must have that balance in a team. Look for that balance when betting.

THE DEFENSIVE LINE

The defensive line's job is to attack the quarterback and also to be the first line of defense against the run. Generally, there may be three or four men on the line, depending on the defense the coach favors.

Most defenses run 4-3 or 3-4, which means that there are four down linemen and three linebackers, or three down linemen and four linebackers. Or they may shift from position to position.

Nowadays there's usually a nose tackle who is in line with the center, ready to bull past him to get to the quarterback. Sometimes with him is another tackle and a defensive end, or two defensive ends.

The ends cut in from the outside, attempting to rush past the running backs trying to block for the quarterback. On passing downs, the defensive ends try and hit the quarterback from the side, creating fumbles. They'll come in from his strong side, the direction he's passing the ball, or they'll come in from his blindside, which is the area his back is to. When he's hit in the blindside, it will mean a fumble and sometimes an injury.

Sometimes safeties move up to the defensive line to put more pressure on the quarterback. They may stay there or fake a safety blitz, an all out attack on the quarterback from the defensive line, leaving the receivers covered only man-to-man or not covered at all. Blitzes are gambles, and against a quarterback with a slow release they often work.

Since the defensive line is so fluid, it works in conjunction with the linebackers. Often the two aspects of the defense are interchangeable, with the linebackers moving up to the line on certain plays.

This fluidity adds to the strength of the defensive line. The offensive line is burdened enough without having to be constantly on the lookout for another player two smashing through. When that happens, the quarterback is pressured into making an error, or the offensive linemen, in desperation, hold and are penalized.

To me, the defense, with its line and its fluidity is really the creative part of NFL football. Offenses are pretty stagnant, but on defense, there can be all sorts of elegant combinations.

The personnel doesn't have to be static either. Unlike the offensive linemen who are trained to handle the pass rush and to open holes for the runners, the defensive line can be changed on passing downs and then again on rushing downs.

Certain players are tremendous against the run but only so-so against the pass. On passing downs the defensive line can be altered for pass rushers, linebackers can be removed, and the entire defense set up for the pass.

In order to have this fluidity, the team must have two things. First of all, the players competent enough to carry out their specific assignments, and secondly, a coach who know what to do about defense. Again, watch to see how a club fills its gaps during trades or the draft, what its priorities are. And follow the games on TV, and watch the defense carefully.

LINEBACKERS

As we have seen, linebackers often work in conjunction with the defensive line. And they work as a unit as well. The key linebacker is the middle linebacker , which, in a 4-3 defense is the linebacker who stands between the other two. In many defenses, he is the captain of the defensive unit, and calls the defense for the team, in the same way that a quarterback calls the offense.

Some middle linebackers are very mobile and are terrific on pass defense. Normally, the middle linebacker's assignment may be to cover the running back coming out of the backfield on a pass play. If the running back stays in to block, he may change his assignment and rush the passer. Of course, this is not always the case, and different teams use their linebackers in different ways. A linebacker other than the middle one may cover a running back - it depends on the philosophy of the coaching staff.

Linebackers basically have two important functions. The first is to shut down the run. One of the greatest of all linebackers, Dick Butkus of the Chicago Bears, was considered by many the best linebacker ever to do this. When a running back at full speed came to the immovable object, Butkus, the old riddle of the irresistible force meeting the immovable object was answered. The running back stopped as if he hit a concrete wall.

Then their function, on passing plays, is to cover a runner out of the backfield, and to rush the passer. With a good head start from behind the defensive line, a powerful linebacker can get up a good head of steam and is awfully difficult to stop. His mere approach can destroy the quarterback's timing, and if the quarterback can't see him coming, the situation is worse. He hears the footsteps and knows he may be hit from the blindside. Often, hearing those footsteps, the quarterback eats the ball, that is, tucks the ball securely to his body and falls in a fetal position to absorb the least amount of punishment.

Linebackers like Lawrence Taylor of the New York Giants, one of the greatest to play the game, are extremely mobile. They may line up anywhere in the defensive backfield, or move up to the line as a defensive lineman or end. Lawrence Taylor coming in from an angle after lining up at the end position is a thing of beauty to watch, if you're rooting for the Giants or just following the game.

If you're the QB, it is striking fear in your heart. This guy is fast and strong and can hit, and you better get that ball released fast. Pity the poor guy looking to pass the ball, looking for an open receiver and knowing that Taylor is coming for him, and has already breezed past the lineman, knocked over the blocking back and is breathing down his neck.

Like the quarterback on the offense, the great linebacker is a star and is readily recognizable. Unlike the offensive linemen, the fans can see just what damage he's doing. He stands out. When he doesn't accomplish what he's supposed to, that can be seen also, but generally only by the coaches or the close TV camera lens, which will show the linebacker on the ground in a heap and the pass going away for a big gainer.

As we said before, the linebackers work best as a unit. Each has a certain responsibility on every play, and if they carry out their duties correctly, the offense can be shut down. The passer will be hurried and the pass will go incomplete or be intercepted. Or if its a running play, there will be a short gain of a yard or two or no gain at all. And the running back will get up and feel a bit queasy after a strong hit.

Where there are two competent linebackers and a third who's weak, the offense may take advantage of this situation, concentrating on the territory the weak linebacker is covering, going after him time and time again. The the defense has to shift things around, and it upsets the defense as a whole and makes it vulnerable.

Along with reading about linebackers, make it a point in watching a game to concentrate on them, to see how they've been functioning, to see whether a long gain, either by pass or run, is the fault of the linebackers. This will give you an insight into one of the key aspects of any defense, and may determine a bet for or against the team and its defense.

THE SAFETIES AND THE CORNERBACKS

Of all the players on the team, with the exception of the kickers, these men are generally the smallest. Size has to give way to speed, because their duty is to prevent the big gain in football, the pass that is caught and run for 20 yards and more. Often they appear naked out there, running one-on-one with a shifty speedy receiver, with the ball sailing towards them.

That is the ultimate test for the cornerback or safety. Can he keep up with the receiver? Can he bat away the pass? It seems as if every eye in the stadium is watching him when this is about to happen, and millions of others are watching it on the TV tube.

Along with speed, these men must have superb self-confidence. A cornerback can't question his ability and last very long in the NFL. And if he gets burned on one play, he has to regroup and be out there doing his best on the next play.

Along with the confidence, the best of the cornerbacks, for example, men like Lester Hayes or Ronnie Lott, have a certain toughness almost bordering sadism. They punish their quarries, and they make sure that the guy who just caught the ball knows that he's been hit hard and will get punished again if he's in their territory.

Part of their job is to make the receiver gun-shy. Often, in the middle of the field, on crossing patterns, receivers hear "footsteps", and drop passes they ordinarily would catch. They know they're about to take a good hit.

There are safeties who have made hitting an art, who time their hit for the very moment that the man they're covering has caught the ball.

Then the hit!

It's perfectly legal, whereas hitting the receiver before the catch is pass interference. But getting in that hit at the precise moment that the ball lands in the hands of the receiver can cause all sorts of mayhem.

First, it can just be an incomplete pass. Or the referee may label it a complete catch and then when the hit comes, the ball is jarred loose and it becomes a fumble.

And now, no matter has happened, the receiver feels that bit of fear creeping up, knowing that on the next crossing pattern, that same safety is going to be there ready to deliver his shot.

That's why a lot of receivers head upfield the minute the ball lands in their hands, even before they have full control of it. They don't want to be in a helpless situation when they get tackled. And by doing this, they often are running without the ball, which by now has bounced out of their hands and is rolling on the turf, up for grabs.

With their big hits, the cornerbacks and safeties can make all sorts of things happen. However, they are not only dependent upon one another to make certain that the proper zones are covered, but they are dependent in many ways on the pass rush their club is able to put on the quarterback.

In the NFL, any quarterback, given the proper amount of time, will be able to zing that ball right into the mitts of a receiver who is open. Just give him the time. But if there's a strong pass rush that hurries his throw, or he has to scramble around and throw off balance, or he knows he has to get rid of that ball before getting hit by a defensive end or linebacker, we have a totally different story.

Now the chances are that the ball won't be accurate or even to an open receiver. If you watch TV you'll be amazed how time and time again a quarterback will throw to an end who's double or even triple-teamed.

Why? He had to get rid of the ball somehow, and stupidly he threw it to this end. He could have thrown it away, but even that decision takes time with the linebacker about to give him a whack that might send an ordinary man to the hospital for several months.

With this kind of pass rush, the cornerbacks and the safeties are able to shine even brighter. They'll defend against the receivers much more easily, and they'll get more interceptions. Their position at these times is a reactive position, reacting to what is going on in the backfield as the quarterback is rushed.

Often a solid rush on the quarterback makes up for mediocre cornerbacks. If you are betting on a team that can't mount a pass rush, and has a weak secondary, then you are going to be punished because that team is leaky and will give up a ton of points.

Particularly in under and over bets, look for teams with a great pass rush and a solid secondary. Then you know that there's one team on the field that won't be giving up many points.

4. OTHER IMPORTANT ASPECTS

Offenses and defense aren't the only aspects of NFL football. There's also the kicking game, where the punter is a defensive player and the field goal kicker an offensive player. There are the specialty teams, which can often break a game wide open. Then there is the matter of turnovers, where one team makes a mistake by giving up the ball to the other team. Other factors that play key roles in the game are injuries, drugs and finally, the weather.

We'll cover all of these in the following sections.

THE KICKING GAME

The kickers are a special group, separate from the other players. Kickers only have to do one thing well, kick the ball. They don't have to tackle or run or catch or throw passes. They can be men of short stature and of frail build. Their job is not to take or give punishment. They are loners, who practice by themselves. But they are an important part of the game, and often the outcome depends upon their skill. Let's first examine the field goal kickers.

THE FIELD GOAL KICKERS

All of us who have ever watched pro football are familiar with the situation. The score is 21-20 and there's about 15 seconds left on the clock. The offense has driven the ball down to the 30 yard line, and with those 15 ticks remaining on the clock, and his team behind by 1 point, out comes the field goal kicker.

He trots out alone, goes into the huddle with his teammates but stays aloof from them even in the huddle. Then the team breaks out of the huddle, and lines up. The reserve quarterback stays back with the kicker, to hold the ball for him.

"It's going to be a 38 yard attempt", the sportscaster breathlessly informs the public listening or watching the game on TV. This is it. If the field goal is made, the kicker is a hero. If its missed, he's a bum. There's no place to hide. It's his play all the way.

The other team has three or four players in the center of the line with their hands up in the air, jumping up and down. The kicker takes two or three steps back, moves to one side and is ready. He nods to the man who's going to be holding the ball. The reserve quarterback barks the count, the ball is snapped by the center, held by the reserve quarterback. The kicker approaches the ball, put his shoe to it, the ball sails toward the goalposts, the game is on the line...

At that moment the most important player on the field is that field-goal kicker. Everything that happened up to that final moment has no importance. It doesn't really matter that one team scored 21 points and is leading or that the other team has scored 20 points and is behind.

The kick will decide the game, and negate the efforts of 60 minutes of sweat and anguish on the part of one of the teams.

Players like Morten Andersen of New Orleans relish these moments. They're kickers at the top of their profession and they live for the pressure. They know they can perform. If anyone on that field needs what is known as self-confidence it is the field goal kicker.

He is a breed apart. He may not even be an American, and more and more field goal kickers are imported from Europe or Central or South America, where their style of soccer kicking can be used in the NFL. What they have in common are powerful legs. A solid field-goal kicker adds an additional dimension to a team's offense. Without him, a drive to the opponent's 30 or 35 yard line means nothing more than a punt, on fourth down, hoping to contain the other team deep in their own territory.

But with the good field goal kicker, that same drive means three extra points on the scoreboard. Those 3 points add up during a game. We now see games in the NFL where one team's output of points is wholly made up of 3 point field goals.

Many games are won by 3 points or less. And to those who bet on NFL games, those three pointers can mean the difference between covering the spread or losing.

So the field goal kickers bear careful study.

At one time, the main difference between the NFL and college game was in the placement of the goal posts. In college they were 10 yards behind the end line, while in the NFL they were on the goal line. If you ever see photos or movies of the old NFL games, you'll see those goal posts padded at the goal line, with receivers and backs running around with the defensive players, all trying to avoid getting suckered into running into them.

The rule was changed because field goals were getting automatic in the NFL, and teams stopped going for touchdowns but concentrated on getting good field position, trotting out their field-goal kicker and getting those three points. The fans did not like that. Even though the game is called football, and was basically at its beginning a game where the foot counted more than the hand, it was evolved into a game of passing and running, with the foot becoming secondary.

And to the millions of fans the NFL had accumulated, field goals were boring things, made often by men whom the fans did not really think of as real football players.

So the rules were changed, and the goal posts moved back 10 yards, to make the field goal a more difficult score. And so it has become. There is a big difference between a 40 and 50 yard try. That extra ten yards stops a lot of 3 pointers.

Along with that rule change, another was instituted. In the old days, if a field goal was missed, the other team took the ball on offense from its own 20 yard line no matter where the kick was tried from. Thus, it paid to try 50 and even 60 yard field goals, because the team knew the other side would be getting the ball in poor field position, even if the field goal was missed.

It was better than a punt, because a punt couldn't put points on the board, while any desperate field goal try might. And teams with players like Rick Dempsey knew the guy was capable of 60 yard field goals, even though he was missing half his kicking foot.

Now the rule has been changed so that only field goal attempts from 20 or fewer yards in goes back to the 20 yard line, with the other team taking the ball after a miss.

From any distance greater than 20 yards out, the other team gets the ball after a miss at the previous line of scrimmage. If the ball is on the 35 yard line of the opponents, and the offensive team tries a field goal and misses, the other team gets the ball at that same 35 yard line.

Now coaches are much more cautious about trying long field goals, for they're giving the other team fine field position if they miss.

Of course, it the situation is desperate, they may still try the long field goal. For example, if there's only about a minute left on the clock and it looks as if they won't get the ball back on offense, they may try a 55 yarder, no matter what field position they give the other team, if that kick will tie or win the game for them.

Usually, the man who's the field goal kicker is also the point-after kicker in the NFL. While a point after kick is almost automatic after a touchdown is scored, its not truly automatic, and many teams have lost games by that one point margin due to a missed point after a kick. When betting on NFL games, if we get a gift by a missed kick, fine. But we shouldn't count on it.

We have to assume that after a touchdown, there will be 7 points put up on the board.

In close defensive struggles, the difference may very well be the field goal kicker, and the team that has the best one may rely on him to win the game. With high powered offenses that can score the TD, the field goal kicker takes on less importance.

If a field goal will determine the outcome of the game, then you're in bad shape if you've laid 4 or more points on the game, because, at best, your team will win by three or fewer points. In the tight defensive struggles, you've got to be careful laying the points, because you may lose straight-up as well as not cover the spread. Lay points when you won't be sweating out a single point making the difference between cashing in and tearing up your tickets.

Of course, a lot of that may be hindsight, and it's easy to see these things after the game is over. But generally, lay points when there's a team that can put points up on the board, so that you have a cushion.

Don't be laying 4 or 5 points with a team that relies basically on its field goal kicker, and pray that somehow the team will win by two field goals. There will be better spots to look at in any week's schedule.

PUNTERS

We usually see a lot of kicks when a team can't move the ball well, and then out comes the punter, trying somehow to keep the other team at bay with a long kick. Statistics keep track of the length of the actual punt, but there are also stats on the net yardage of kicks, and that's more important.

There are punters who can kick for 50 to 60 yards but the return man is running it back 30 yards and the net is hardly anything. Or there are kickers, who, when punting from the other team's 45 yard line, send the ball into the end zone, so that the opponent now has a first down on its own 20 yard line without even having to handle the ball.

In this case, the punter hasn't done his job. When a team is in the other squad's territory, from the 49 yard line down, it is the punter's job to either kick the ball in bounds within the goal line and the 10 yard line, forcing the return man to make a decision about whether or not to handle the ball in heavy traffic and possibly cough up a fumble, or to let the ball roll where it will, so that it ends up near the goal line.

In either case the team receiving the punt is in a deep hole. What a good punter does is *lengthen* the field for the other team.

When the ball is within its own 10 yard line, the receiving team is practically forced to run the ball, for a badly thrown pass can invite disaster in the form of an interception that may very well be run in for a score. A field 95 yards long is a long field for any offensive team.

The key in many football situations is to have the team with the ball consume as much yardage as possible in order to score points. Teams that constantly have the ball in good field position (from their own 40 yard line forward) are apt to cash in on several drives and put points on the board.

Moving them to their own 20 is much better, but best of all is having them with their backs to their own goal line with upwards of 90 yards to go. Often that situation is in the hands of a punter.

When a punter is kicking in a purely defensive mode, that is, when his team is up against its own goal line and he wants to air that ball out to give them some breathing room, it is usually more important to kick the ball high and moderately deep rather than to kick it deep but low .

With the rule that only the defensive ends can go downfield before the ball is kicked, long hang time (the time the ball is in the air before the receiving team fields it) gives his teammates the opportunity to run downfield and nail the punt return man.

Many times the result of a high kick is a fair catch, where the punt return man gives up the option of running back the punt.

Having a punt return man make a fair catch gives the kicking team two distinct advantages.

First of all, the man catching the ball is usually one of the fastest if not the fastest man on their squad, and he creates a dangerous situation for his opponents when he has the ball in his hands. That is now completely negated.

And secondly, if he is forced to make a fair catch, he can very well fumble the ball, with the opportunity for the kicking team to recover and start a new drive in much better field position than they had before.

Thus you can see the importance of the punter. However, though teams throughout the NFL lack good kickers, they don't often draft highly for them. There are exceptions, of course, such as the Raiders taking Ray Guy, who was their punter for many years, in the first round of the draft.

A punter is a key player on the team. He is often overlooked because he doesn't put points directly on the board the way a field goal kicker, a quarterback, running back or receiver does, but he's responsible for setting up situations where points can be scored. In the worst scenario, he's there to give his own team some breathing room when they're in a hole.

In bad weather, when both teams may be bogged down in snow

or rain or mud, the kicker's job takes on even more importance. If you know a game is going to be played in those conditions, then you must carefully examine the respective punters on the teams before making an intelligent decision about the game.

THE SPECIALTY TEAMS

As football became more and more compartmentalized the specialty teams came into focus. In the old days the team about to take the field for the offense usually was there when the other team kicked off. Then they stayed on the field. It is analogous to the situation in the NBA where the same team that starts the game with the tip-off stays in there as the first team.

However, in the NFL today, this isn't the case. The specialty team receives the ball on all kickoffs and then leaves the field, and the offense moves in to take over.

Who makes up a specialty team? Usually veterans on their way out, rookies, second stringers and the like, along with a couple of speedy running backs if the team is to receive the ball. If the team is kicking away, then tackling prowess may be substituted for speed.

Specialty teams are also used in fourth down situations, where the ball is about to be punted away, or a field goal is attempted. In these situations an entire new squad isn't put into play, but several new members may join the action. Their main focus, however, is in receiving kickoffs or defending against the team receiving kickoffs.

Most of the defenders are taught to cover lanes to prevent an opening by the man with the ball. On the other hand, the team getting the ball tries to set up a wedge to block out all players in the runner's path. Often the runner goes off on his own, if he has terrific field vision and can spot openings.

When a team receives a kickoff and immediately runs it in for a touchdown, it is a great boost to the team. They've scored in a matter of seconds. They've given their offense a rest, and not subjected them to any kind of punishment. The other team now has to handle the ball on a kickoff with all the bad things that can develop from this.

What bad things? If the ball isn't handled cleanly, it can lead to a fumble deep in the receiving teams' territory, which may result in

80

extremely poor field position, or worse, loss of he ball altogether, with the other team now in possession deep in their territory.

A good coach should have competent specialty teams. A poor coach will have sloppy or inept specialty teams. This is sometimes pitifully easy to see when watching a game in person or on the TV tube. Missed tackles, penalties, fumbles, or a receiver not knowing what to do with a kickoff that sails deep into the endzone. That is a terrible mistake, when a receiver get the ball five yards into the endzone and instead of downing it, runs it out. Usually, before he does this, he will look befuddled, halfway put one knee down and then he'll take off.

In this case, you can blame the coach. The receiver should know exactly what to do when the ball goes in deep in the endzone. He should drop to one knee and down it, so that his team can take over on its own 20 yard line. When he runs it out in this situation, the odds are that he'll be tackled within his own 10 yard line or he'll fumble the ball.

When I see this, I usually see a hole in the whole coaching philosophy of the team he's playing for and I may lose interest in putting my money on a team so poorly coached.

When there are penalties for blocking below the waist, that's another sign of bad coaching. The team handling the kickoff should have been drilled and trained in what is proper procedure. It should be second nature to them. In the NFL you can't afford to have a bunch of renegades on the kickoff receiving team, making up the play as they go along, ad libbing, so to speak. They should know what they're doing and shouldn't make foolish and stupid mistakes. Mistakes happen in the sport, with bodies slamming all over the place, but there's never an excuse for stupid mistakes.

Often, the coach will put his speediest man back to receive the kickoff or the punt. These breakaway fast runners are dangerous. They can make long gains, or given a couple of breaks and small openings, they can go all the way for a TD. Not only does this give a team fast points, but sometimes one of these quick touchdowns can change the whole momentum of a game, lift a team's spirits in a way that no other single play can do.

This extra scoring dimension is an important consideration when betting on games. Look for the speedy runners in competently coached specialty teams. And also look to avoid betting on teams where the coaching is sloppy, and the specialty team's mistakes will cost the team points.

Like kickers, when the weather is really bad, the specialty teams will be on the field more than usual, fielding punts for example, and that's when they can make all the difference. It's another factor to look at carefully.

TURNOVERS

A turnover occurs when the team in possession of the ball gives it away to the other team before it has used up its full four downs. For example, on a kickoff, the man getting the ball fumbles it and the other team recovers. Or a ball comes loose from a runner on first down and the other team recovers. Or a pass is intercepted. Or a receiver catches a pass, runs a few yards, takes a hard hit and coughs up the ball.

There are a lot of ways turnovers occur. Sometimes its as simple as a bad exchange between the center and the quarterback. Whatever way it happens, when it happens to the team you've bet on, you're screaming and carrying on and getting as many new gray hairs as the coach watching all this.

Turnovers are potent forces and often are determining factors in close games. It's a pleasure when your team forces the turnover; a disaster when your team makes the turnover.

Stats are kept on turnovers. Publications such as Mort Olshan's *Gold Sheet* published out of Los Angeles, gives the ratio of turnovers in + and - forms.

A plus is a takeaway, that is, the team caused more turnovers than it had. A minus sign stands for more turnovers than caused. This is valuable information worth knowing and it might pay to get your hands on the *Gold Sheet* to see just where the teams stand as far as turnovers are concerned.

Inept teams have a lot of turnovers. Badly coached teams have the same problem. Teams with the minus sign hanging around their necks are usually losing teams, because the accumulation of fumbles, interceptions and other mistakes is just too much of a millstone to carry.

On the other hand, there are teams that are in the minus column that still win a lot of games and cover spreads. These are teams with daring offenses, teams that take chances.

The Pittsburgh Steelers in the 1970s were like this, as were the Raiders over many years. The Raiders went for the big gain, the bomb. They weren't a team to grind out wins. Their quarterbacks threw a lot of interceptions, their runners went all out. They played hard and they made a lot of turnovers. But they won anyway.

A statistic is kept on a quarterback's touchdowns as against his interceptions. When you see the interceptions outweigh the touchdowns, you not only have a questionable QB, you have the basis of a minus sign as far as turnovers are concerned.

Turnovers have the power to make a defensive unit turn into an offensive unit, and thus punish the team they are playing against. When making bets, you can't afford to play against two offenses, in essence. You must weigh this factor carefully.

When you come up against a mediocre team with a minus factor in turnovers it will pay to lay money and points against the team. If the spread isn't too high, there are good spots for you to invest in.

INJURIES

No matter how good a ballplayer is , when he's injured his talent disappears and he can end up as a liability to the team. Or he becomes gun shy, afraid to take or give the hits he normally makes with impunity.

If his player is a quarterback, he may throw the whole team upside down. There will be a lot of holding calls on the offensive line desperate to protect the QB at all costs. More pressure is put on the running backs staying to to protect him. If the QB is hit and is in pain, he will be snapping at his teammates, causing dissension, a sure way to lose games.

When following a game or looking at the stats, I look at statistics, especially those concerning penalties as a result of holding. Holding to me signifies that there's trouble somewhere, perhaps an unreported injury to a key player.

In NFL any injury theoretically must be reported to the press.

There are basically three types of injury or to be more precise, statuses of injured players.

The first is **doubtful**, which means that there is doubt as to whether or not the player will be able to suit up and get in the game. Generally, this category is put in to cover the coach, because he will play the injured player. But if he can't , he's covered, according to the rules of the NFL.

The second category is **probable**. The player is not as badly injured as the doubtful one, but still he's injured and will probably be in the game. However, if he's a key player, a quarterback or linebacker for example, just how badly hurt is he? He may be able to play, but at what effectiveness? The same holds true for the doubtful player.

In football, you can't run and hide from contact. You can't substitute one skill for another. If you're a quarterback you can't use an injured throwing arm. If you're a linebacker, you need mobility and if that knee is acting up again after a big hit the week before, you can't put in two new legs. Thus, we have to be aware of all reported injuries.

For example, if a team reports doubtful and probable injuries to a couple of key players and there's no loss in their skill the next game, we can pretty well disregard these categories.

But if another team's doubtful linebacker screws up his position and the other team ran all over him the week before, we have a wholly different situation. The linebacker has become a liability to the team.

We may be able to get in a bet here, all things being equal, since the oddsmakers haven't really counted on his injury and the line isn't changed to penalize the team that's playing against the weakened linebacker. That's a good spot to get money down on.

The last category is the harshest, as far as injuries is concerned. That's **definitely out**. The injured player won't be playing. Period.

Now we have to ask ourselves several basic questions. First of all, how important is that player? Can he be replaced without loss of strength on the team? If he can't be replaced, is this squad capable of playing over their heads to compensate for his loss?

We must also look at the line and see just how much compensation to the lost player's team the oddsmakers are giving.

Is the change in the spread sufficient to make up for the lost player? If a bet on the team that is intact a good bet considering the change in odds? Is the team without the key player still a good bet, considering all the points we're getting?

As a general rule, I don't like to bet on a team that has lost a key player to injuries. The team might or might not be able to compensate for the loss. I don't like to guess in these situations. If I feel that the loss is an important one, and that the other team hasn't been penalized enough in the line, then I go with the other team.

When a quarterback is injured and out of play, we have to examine the substitute.

If the backup QB is a seasoned veteran, he may be able to step in and continue the system without much loss to the team. If the backup QB however is a youngster fresh out of college, with little experience, then I'm going against this guy and his team. The fans will be rooting for the kid to do well, but after a couple of good licks by the opposing middle linebacker or some crazed safety on a "safety blitz," it won't matter to him what the fans are yelling. He'll be shell-shocked and ineffective.

On occasions there are exceptions to this situation, where a young quarterback comes in an plays a helluva game and establishes himself. But these are rare events and most of the time the QB is welcomed into the NFL with some bruised ribs and a concussion to think about the next time he starts calling signals.

If a first-line runner is injured, it is usually a serious situation for the team. Rarely can a substitute fill in properly, and now there is greater emphasis on the passing game to compensate for the loss of running back, and the equally damaging loss to a balanced attack. Now the defense can key on the passing rush, and this can destroy the complete rhythm of the game.

What the bettor must look out for is the difference between the actual value of a player to a team when that player is injured. Often the local media will hype up the talents of players because the fans want to hear about the team they're rooting for and even mediocre players will be thrust into the limelight. A player's abilities may be trumpeted to the sky, but his performance may leave much to be desired.

Having built up this particular player, the media now finds that he's injured and that the team will be hurting. The betting public eats this up, and swallows the whole story, and the line changes radically. However, you don't have to swallow these hypes and must display cool judgment when you evaluate the situation.

On the other hand, if a really key player has been injured and is out of play, the media may trumpet the team spirit, with others ready to rise to great heights to take this star's place.

Again, that might not be the situation at all. The backup quarterback may be inexperienced and a poor team leader. The backup running back has previously been used in blocking situations and now he's given the ball. If he gains two yards, it's a big run for him. Either way, good or bad, don't believe the hype but make your own decisions as to the value of the missing player or players.

And if your judgment tells you to step in with both fists stuffed with cash to take advantage of an incorrect line, do so. Injuries can create wonderful spots for a good play.

DRUGS

For a long time there has been disagreement between the management and players over proper drug testing. Certainly this will have to be resolved at some point. Drugs have been shown to be prevalent on pro sports, and the NFL should be no exception.

A player on drugs, particularly one like cocaine, is a liability to his team. His teammates may enforce their own code of silence, and not reveal his addiction but every time he suits up, that's a minus for the team. The other players may start to resent him, and this will cause dissension.

If it's a running back who can't get going on that first step anymore after a half of play as his need for drugs kicks in, or the high he's been experiencing has worn off, if he can't make a decent block, he's exposing his teammates not only to defeat, but to possible physical harm.

A receiver may be hyper on drugs for part of the game, then fall into a depression of both spiritual, and physical proportions. He'll be fumbling when hit, he'll not make the proper cuts, he'll forget the count and the pattern he's supposed to run. He'll bring chaos to the passing attack.

The NFL of course would like to see the league drug-free but with all the drugs available, with all the big money paid, with the highs the players need for each game, its merely a time bomb ready to go off. It's anyone's guess as to how many players are on drugs, but if you see players having brilliant first halves and dead second ones, if you see an inordinate amount of fatigue where there shouldn't be any, if players appear to play stupidly on the field, then you have to be on the lookout for drugs.

You can't afford to bet on a drug-ridden team. It will lack any sort of consistency. You won't know what it's capable of doing from one week to another, let alone one quarter to another.

IS THERE CHEATING IN THE NFL?

In the old days, when the American Football League was a separate entity, there was talk at times of games being thrown or shaved, and every once in a while, a game was **taken off the board**.

This means that the bookmakers refused to take bets on the contest. They were leery of something. Perhaps they heard rumors or they really knew something. I don't believe anything has ever been proved or evidence that would stand up in court submitted about thrown games in pro football.

Today, in the NFL, you can be pretty sure that the games is squeaky clean. If that wasn't the case, the bookies would probably be the first to know, with a sudden influx of money going to one side out of the blue. This rarely happens, and when it does, it's usually some big bettor falling in love with a team's chances, or some well-known tout announcing his periodic "lock of the decade."

Bookmakers throughout the country keep a tight rein on the line, and know just what is happening around America, as far as football action is concerned. And certainly in Las Vegas, the line is watched closely. If anything fishy seemed to be happening, if the line suddenly and dramatically changed, the bookies would know about it, of course, and would begin asking questions. This doesn't happen.

NFL athletes make a lot of money these days and a million dollar a year contract isn't that exceptional anymore.

Just how much money would an athlete need to be bribed? Who knows? And even if someone decided to fix a game, who's he going to bribe? The quarterback? The linebacker? A cornerback? The game is a team game, and one individual can only make so much of a difference.

Of course, if a quarterback goes into the tank, his team is in a lot of trouble. But why would a quarterback do this? He's generally the highest paid player on his club, and his contract depends upon his performance. If you promised him 100 grand to throw the game, then you've got to bet a least that much just to break even. If you pour in 200 grand, it's going to affect the line, and even more money will be a red flag to the bookmakers. Something will be fishy.

There's always talk of bribing the officials, the line judges, referees, etc. But as far as I'm concerned it's just talk.

To sum up. Forget about cheating in the NFL. Concentrate on your picks and bets. Most of the cheating cries come from the constant losers, who are paranoid enough to think there's an entire conspiracy in the NFL, running from top to bottom, from a quarterback to line judge, just to cheat them out of their $50 bet.

WEATHER FACTORS

We've touched on the weather from time to time, and as Mark Twain so wittily said, "Everyone talks about the weather, but nobody does anything about it." Well, we can do something about it. No, we can't change it, but we can certainly take advantage of it in our wagering, and we can study it as a factor in our bets.

Any evening on TV you're going to be able to see the weather in all parts of the country when the weatherman or woman takes out the pointy stick and says "rain forecast for the South, snow for the Northeast," and so forth.

If we don't watch the evening news on TV, the local newspaper, if its big enough, will have the weather for the country somewhere in its pages. A newspaper like *USA Today* , which by the way has an excellent sports section well worth reading, will have a full weather map of the United States, with extended forecasts.

Weatherpeople have been wrong a lot, and a great many long term forecasts don't pan out. They talk about sunshine and you wake up to a blizzard, and so forth. Early in the week, you might want to take advantage of the weather conditions before the bookie changes the line. You've studied the weather maps and feel that there's going to be a blizzard in New York, where the Giants are playing the Eagles.

The over-under number is 35, let's say, and you start pouring money into the under bet. With a field that's wet and slippery, with snow falling and a wind howling, this is going to be a game that will end up 10-7 either way, and you don't care which way. You just want a low scoring game.

But so far in advance, you're taking a chance. If you're right, then you probably will have an easy win on that under wager. You've made a smart bet because the number, as the weather turns bad, gets lower and lower as the week goes on.

However, if you're wrong, and the storm passes harmlessly away a hundred miles north of Giants Stadium, and the sunshine beams down on two teams ready to air the ball, you may be eating the bet. You hear about the sunshine, and this depresses you, and by halftime, the Giants are leading 17-13, and you know you're doomed to lose.

So you have a choice. You may want to wait till the last minute to be certain about weather, or you might anticipate it by going along with the meteorologist. If you have a way of being certain about the future weather; either by insight or by following a weather person who's very accurate, then that's a good edge to have over the bookie. If you're not able to predict the weather with any degree of certainty, then you're just gambling and you don't really want to do that.

In domed stadiums, there's no weather factor, and those games must be handicapped strictly on other factors and principles. Also games played in usually sunny climates such as Phoenix and Southern California. Denver on the other hand is very volatile, and blizzards can develop quickly in the Rockies.

If you want to wait till the last minute, you can easily find out the weather in a particular city by simply calling the local airport and asking about the weather there, telling them you're thinking of flying to that city. That's a very simple way to do this, and doesn't necessitate any long-distance calls.

If the weather is really bad, then anything can happen on the playing field, and if one team isn't that much better than the other, anyone can win. A strong wind, bitter cold, a hard rain, falling snow, can play havoc with any play. A sure touchdown becomes a sliding fumble. A pass floats in the air away from the receiver into a safety's hands ten yards away.

A punter lets the football slide through his fingers and it rolls to the goaline where the other team falls on it for an easy touchdown.

As a general rule, take the points and don't give them in terrible weather.

As we wrote, anything can happen and usually does. And the game is generally a low scoring affair.

The one constant can be the running game. A good running back can adjust but still he has to slog through tough yard after tough yard. Even the kicking game can go crazy. In extremely cold weather, the football gains in weight as it travels through the air. Punts can lose distance. Field goals can go awry.

Again, anything can happen. But it still pays to have the superior kicker because you'll need him to get the team out of difficult field positions in a game dominated now by the defense.

See what kind of surface the team is playing on. In wet weather, the artificial turf will turn into a sliding pond, with everyone slipping all over the place. Grass has more traction, but mud will slow everyone down.

Rather than guess about these factors, study previous situations at particular stadiums. What happened the last time the Denver Broncos played in a blizzard at Mile High Stadium? What was the final score? Who won and by how many points? In Foxboro, Mass, how does a bitterly cold day affect the game score? How about Indianapolis? Or Green Bay?

Study the previous games by reading back issues of *Sports Illustrated*, for example, from years before. Or subscribe to a service that will give you back issues of its records of the games. Or watch the games on TV if you can't get back issues. But know just how each stadium and team reacts to inclement weather and you'll be able to make intelligent decisions, and often outthink the and bookmaker.

Now that we've covered the various factors that make up the pro football game, it's time to get down to the nitty gritty, to look at the 10 Winning Strategies for NFL Football Betting.

C. THE 10 WINNING STRATEGIES FOR NFL FOOTBALL BETTING

Up to now, we've gone into all the factors that should be examined when betting on NFL games. We've had an in-depth examination of the official line, so that we can see just how it's made up, what its strengths and weaknesses are.

We now know that the relative strengths and talents of the two teams involved are only a small part of that line. That the line isn't made for the bettors, its made for the bookmakers. Just knowing this is going to make us money.

Study the strategies we're going to show in this section, because they're going to be the difference between winning and losing at NFL football.

1. Don't depend on anyone else's judgment, especially when it come to touts. Use your own judgments and your own logic.

2. There's no magic road to winning bets except study, hard work and proper evaluation of the situation.
Everyone out there is looking for the "magic formula" for winning. They want to key in on the one principle that will make them money. However, there really isn't a single principle; there are any number of factors and principles to be evaluated.

3. Avoid looking at factors that are meaningless. This is an important consideration. I know of handicappers who pour over stats, trying to link winners and losers by the fact that a particular field was natural turf whereas another field was artificial turf. Then they tried to work a formula based on these factors. They many not even be relevant.

Or they're looking at beaten favorites, or beaten underdogs, or teams that have won as home favorites and lost road dogs, or whatever. Forget about all this. These are usually just random meaningless facts.

Remember, the teams don't know about these things. They're out there playing as best they can against a particular opponent. They don't know that they lost on artificial turf the last time they were road dogs, or that they won on natural grass as a road dog. They only know that they won or lost.

Don't get too esoteric or cute with the factors you want to cover. Cover only those that have any true meaning as far as winning or losing is concerned. This will save you a lot of money and a lot of time.

4. Go for consistency. When a team is good, it should remain good barring something unforeseen such as a crippling injury. If the team has bad game one week don't write off the team. On the other hand, a weak team has no reason to improve dramatically without an infusion of new talent. If they have a good game, they'll revert to their level of play the next week.

5. Go against the perceptions of the betting public which are nearly always wrong. A simple example is in principle 4, where a good team has a bad game or vice versa, and the betting public now thinks only of this game the next week. Go against the public. That's the way the bookies make their fortunes and you can also.

6. Lay off games you can't figure out. There's no reason to bet just to have action. Your one reason for betting, as we've drilled over and over again, is to make money.

7. Bet only a few games, those games in which you are confident of victory. The fewer the better. If you find one good game, bet that game. After you've made your selections, rate the game from 1 to 5, with 5 the highest and 1 the lowest.

Then narrow your bets to the "5" games. If you have no "5" games but only a mess of "1" and "2" games, then lay off betting that week. Forget about action.

How do you rate a game as "5"? If the official line deviates at least 3 points from your line. Which brings us to the next critical strategy - making your own line.

8. Make your own line and have confidence in it. Having studied all the factors that make up a line in the NFL, you want to make your own line, which is not for the benefit of the betting public, but for your benefit. It is not there to help the bookies balance the books, but for you to win money from the bookies.

Let's give an example. The New England Patriots are playing Denver at Denver's Mile High Stadium. Denver has a rabid following at home which really lifts their team. New England has been struggling. The bookies install Denver at -10 for the game. You've already weighed all the factors, and you think Denver can win the games, and you've scored it -10 on your line.

What do you do? Lay off the game. The line doesn't have a "crease", that is, it's not incorrect for one reason or another.

That same week, Dallas is playing Washington at home. Dallas has also been struggling with its new young quarterback. But last week he had a brilliant game against the Giants, and pulled off a last-minute victory. Meanwhile, a strong Washington team looked lackluster against San Diego in a game they were favored in by two touchdowns, winning, 13-10.

The bookies make this game Washington -2.

You've evaluated the two teams and their season so far, and if you eliminated the last week's results, you'd favor Washington by at least 9 points.

Here's where you rate this game a "5" and get some good money on Washington. The betting public's perceptions have distorted the line, which has been accommodated for that purpose.

9. Make a list of all the NFL teams and give them a rating in terms of strength. In order to do this you must keep detailed records of how they've performed this season and for the last couple of years. See if the ratings hold up week after week, for about four to six weeks before you start betting money. In other words, be able to win on paper before you commit real money. Don't just jump into action because it's there.

With a comparative rating of teams, your job is a lot easier. If the lowest number connotes the best team (as does the *Gold Sheet*) and Team A is a 3 and Team B, whom they're playing, is a 7, then Team A is theoretically 4 points better than Team B. If Team A is at home, then with the HFA (home field advantage) they are rated as 7 points better than Team B.

If the bookies pretty much agree within one point, then the line can't be bet into. But if they make Team A -3 only, there's a crease in the line, and they're worth betting on against Team B.

However, before you blindly do this, examine the reasoning for only a -3 line. It may be caused by several factors that aren't immediately apparent. There may be an unreported injury, or one of the key players has a nagging injury and can't play up to his potential.

Or some other reason. Here's where you have to have as much information as you possibly can. Maybe the game is a grudge match, and as you examine your records you see that Team A humiliated Team B a year or two ago. Revenge is a great motivator.

Or a trend has come into focus. You must respect trends. Your records indicate that Team A always seems to do badly against Team B at home.

Respect the revenge factor or any other motivator, and certainly respect trends. Don't go against either. As you see, we're adding a complexity to the line's formation. But football betting isn't simple. Very few people can beat the spread. In order to do so, you have to dig deeper.

10. Study and restudy all the factors we've gone into. Look for your spots, where there's either a deviation from the official line on the game, or the over-under number, and bet on your line.

However, before you do this, one final word. Your line will be a comparative one based on the team's talent. Then you'll weigh in motivation, injuries, weather and all the other things we've discussed. Now you come up with a number.

But, at the outset of the season, don't make any cash bets. Wait and see how well you do by making imaginary bets based on your line.

Unless you can win more than 52.38% of the time, you're going to be losing money.

You have to win at least 53% of the time because of the bookie's vig at 11-10. If you can't meet at least that number (53%), don''t put down any real cash. Keep working on your own line, refining and developing it.

If you find that you're able to win 55% of the time, start making bets. If you then find your win percentage drops dramatically, stop betting and re-examine the line.

Don't just crave action. Crave winning money.

D. MONEY AND MONEY MANAGEMENT

Since you'll eventually be betting real money, you must know the facts about the money you're betting in terms of the bookie's vig.

If you win 53% of the time, you're winning 53 games and losing 47 out of theoretical 100 games. It boils down to this: ($100 bets).

53 wins	+$5,300.00
47 losses	- $4,700.00
Bookie's vig	- $470.00
Net win	**+ $130.00**

...$130 profit after a total of $10,000 bet isn't much of a profit, but still, it's a win. If you can do this, you're better than 95% of the people who bet on NFL football.

What we want to do is get a higher win percentage, of at least 55%. If that happens, here's what a theoretical 100 bets at $100 looks like.

55 wins	+$5,500.00
45 losses	-$4,500.00
Bookie's vig	-$450.00
Net win	**+$550.00**

A jump of just two percentage points has given us an additional $420 in profits!

Let's now move to an ideal situation. We are able to win 60% of our games. Here's how our flat bet of $100 played 100 times looks:

60 wins	+$6,000.00
40 losses	-$4,000.00
Bookie's vig	-$400.00
Net win	**+$1,600.00**

We've now own more than 12 times what we did with the same bets, but only winning 53% of the time.

INCREASING OUR NET WINS

For purposes of having net wins clearly, let's assume that we're big bettors and have started with a bankroll of $10,000 for our NFL season. We've not made a bet for three weeks until we were able to theoretically win at least 53% of the time. However, we've made a good line for ourselves and we're winning 55% of the time.

How much should we be betting on any particular game?

To maximize our wins, we should bet 5% of our bankroll. Let's say that our 55% holds up for the season. Here's what our chart would look like with $50 bets:

55 wins	+$27,500.00
45 losses	- $22,500.00
Bookie's Vig	+$2,250.00
Net win	**+ $2,500.00**

Compare that to our theoretical 55% win at a flat $100 a bet, which was just $550.00. Of course, you may be much more comfortable with a smaller bankroll, of, let us say, $1,000, with an average $50 bet per game, Only bet what you can afford to lose, never more.

If our winning percentage increases, we should adjust for this with bigger and bigger bets in terms of the percentage of our total bankroll.

However, before we rush into that casino with our cash gripped in our sweaty hands, a word of caution. It's impossible to sustain a constant winning percentage. We'll have good weeks and bad weeks, but what we want is to be able to keep our bankroll for the long haul.

Let's assume that you've practiced your line until the end of a season without betting, and are satisfied that you can win at least 55% of the time. The new season has begun. What do you do?

Don't come out with $500 bets. Test the results in actual play. It's easy to bet imaginary money; it's another thing to bet real cold cash.

Also, you may have altered your perception of your actual wins, by discounting a couple of losses, thinking, "no, they shouldn't have been bet." It's easy to do this when you're not really betting legal tender.

Start the season with an intact bankroll and begin with no more than 2% of your bankroll on any one game. Let's say you bet two games and won one and lost one, each at $200. Now you're $20 in the hole. Still make those 2% bets.

The next week, both teams win, and you win $400. You've won 3 out of four games you've bet on for a fantastic 75% win ratio. Should you now be thinking of betting at least 30% of your bank-roll on the next week's game? No!!! Whoa, slow down. It's early in the season, and there are great deviations at this point. You bet three games the next week and lose two out of three.

Now you've won four out of 7 games for a 57% win ratio. Still bet the 2% for another week.

The next week, you win two out of four games. Now you've won 6 out of 11 games. Or 54.5% of the games. You haven't won much money, and you would have won much more betting $500 a game instead of $200, but you can't anticipate wins. Let's assume that by the sixth week of the season, you find yourself with a steady 55.5% win ratio. Now you can start increasing the bets.

Remember, when we showed you the way to maximize your wins, it's a dangerous and risky business. What happened before should happen again, but there's nothing written in stone that this mighty happen. And you've got to protect yourself against a dangerous losing streak where all your profits are quickly lost in two disastrous betting weeks. Don't be ready to jump to the maximum.

Our best advice is this. Start with 2% of your bankroll for the first three weeks. If your percentage of wins holds at least 55%, move up to 3% and then 4% of your bankroll. Then, if it still holds, get up to 5%. Don't go above this figure.

At the end of the NFL season, add up your percentage of wins. If it has been 56%, for example, then you'll have more confidence the next season, and move up to the 5% much more quickly.

If you fall below the 52.38%, then you have to be careful. If you are winning only 50% of the games, stop betting and re-examine your line. If it lingers around 52%, you can stay in there, because you'll be losing some vig, but your main bankroll will be pretty much intact.

Hold onto that bankroll. Make it last. Don't just crave action. Pick your spots. You may ask, "just how many games a week should I bet?" Bet as many as you're confident about. No more, no less. If you don't like any games on any particular weekend, don't make a bet. Be smart.

Now, just how much of a bankroll should you have to start the NFL season. It depends on your financial status.

Don't bet with money you can't afford to lose, for any reason whatsoever. If you have extra money, then use whatever is comfortable for you as your NFL seasonal bankroll. If it's $1,000, you're going to have to be comfortable making $20 bets at the outset. Don't risk losing that bankroll with wild bets on hunches. Hunches don't win anything but heartaches. Stick to the principles and strategies we've outlined, and you should do O.K.

If your winning percentage increases, then increase your bets. If you're winning 55% of the time and fall to 52%, decrease your bets. Lower your wagers when on a losing streak. If your percentage of wins falls to 50% or less, stop betting till you figure out what is wrong with your line.

If you can't raise that percentage any higher that season, even with imaginary bets, stop betting. Hold onto your bankroll for another season. In the off-season, away from the hectic schedule of games, the media hype and everything else that goes on during NFL football season, study the past season's play with a clear head.

Follow the advice in this section, and you'll be acting smarter than all those losers you'll be seeing in the casinos. They want action and they want to gamble. You don't want either.

You want to win. You want to beat the bookie.

But you've got to have the bankroll in order to bet and win the bookie's money and if you've foolishly lost it by week 3 by wild and crazy bets, going against our principles, and based primarily on hunches.

You're out of money and you're out of action. Having calmed down and now studied and applied our principles, while the teams you would have bet on win and win, it'll do you no good, if you can't make a bet.

Money management is of extreme importance. It's not only managing your money to squeeze the most out of your wins, but it's a matter of preserving your capital so that, when your winning streak starts, you'll have the cash to make the correct bets.

E. TEAMS OF THE NFL

In the next sections, we'll examine the structure of the NFL, and give just a brief synopsis of each team. We're not going to cover the personnel of the individual squads because these change from season to season. We want simply to give you a feel for the teams and their places in the respective division and conferences.

AMERICAN FOOTBALL CONFERENCE

At one time the American Football League (AFL) was a bitter competitor of the NFL. However, a merger was forged between the two leagues, and most of the teams that came into the NFL this way ended up in the American Football Conference (AFC).

There are three divisions within the AFC, the Eastern, Central and Western. Some of the old-line NFL teams, such as the Cleveland Browns and Pittsburgh Steelers, moved to the AFC when the merger was effected, breaking up some traditional rivalries.

There is talk of realignment of the NF, with changes within divisions. Sometimes, as we will see in the NFC, a team such as Atlanta or New Orleans is in the wrong geographical location for its particular division. However, in the AFC, the geographical considerations are pretty correct.

Eastern Division

BUFFALO BILLS
The Buffalo Bills were an original member of the old AFL, and they play in one of the smallest markets in the country in terms of TV coverage. The games are also broadcast in Canada, and the Bills have a large following there as well as upstate New York.

Over the years they've had some great runners, and perhaps the greatest of them all, O.J. Simpson. Depending upon their personnel, the Bills have good years and mediocre years, but up to now they've never put it all together to get to the Super Bowl.

One of the trends to look at with this team is the poor record against the spread when playing at Miami.

INDIANAPOLIS COLTS
In 1984 the Colts were moved from Baltimore by their owner, Bob Irsay, ending a great tradition. In Baltimore the Colts had some legendary teams, led by the magnificent Johnny Unitas, who came off the sandlots to lead the Colts to tremendous seasons. But that's all in the past now.

In the shadows of history now stand their two immortal games, the NFL title game against the New York Giants in 1958, which the Colts won in overtime, 23-17, and which many followers of the game consider the finest game ever played in the NFL. It certainly impressed the American public, which discovered just how thrilling NFL football can be and heralded in the glory days of the sport.

The other big game was a loss in the third Super Bowl in 1968

100

to the Jets, led by Joe Namath. This game paved the way for the unification of the two leagues and established the AFC teams as equal to the NFC teams.

In Indianapolis, the Colts were greeted with open arms, as new franchises usually are. They've put together some fine seasons there before good crowds.

Like the Patriots, the Colts have problems covering against the Dolphins, whether playing at home or in Miami.

MIAMI DOLPHINS

The Dolphins come into the AFL in 1966 and under coach Don Shula, utilizing talent such as Bob Griese at quarterback, with runners like Larry Csonka, Jim Kiick and Mercury Morris, together with a "no name" defense, they reached the Super Bowl in 1971, and the next year were undefeated through the season including the playoffs and Super Bowl, the only team ever to do this in the NFL.

With the death of Joe Robbie, the team's destinies have passed to his family. No longer playing in the Orange Bowl, the Dolphin's new home is Joe Robbie Stadium.

NEW ENGLAND PATRIOTS

When they originally came into the AFL, they were known as the Boston Patriots,.but with their move to Foxboro, the Patriots try and command a regional, rather than a strictly Boston following.

In 1985, they finally made it to the Super Bowl but took a terrible beating from the Chicago Bears. The bettors are familiar with the fact that the Patriots have traditionally been a streaky team, and in 1985 they covered 14 times in a row!

NEW YORK JETS

The Jets, then known as the Titans, were one of the original group that made up the AFL. By 1963 they were owned by Sonny Werblin, who hired Weeb Ewbank as their coach, and with the advent of "Broadway Joe" Namath for the 1965 season, the Jets, now installed in their new home at Shea Stadium, caught the imagination of the public. Namath bragged that he'd beat the Baltimore Colts and the 1968 Super Bowl, and he lived up to his promise.

This victory established the AFL as an equal of the the old NFL

In recent years the Jets have had a tendency to weaken towards the end of the season. Now playing in the Giant's Stadium in New Jersey, we should note that they have a tough time covering against the spread during the tail end of the season.

Central Division

CINCINNATI BENGALS

The Bengals first coach in the old AFL was Paul Brown, one of those legendary men who have left their mark in the annals of NFL history. After his retirement the team had trouble finding itself, but has made it into the Super Bowl twice in the 1980s, both times losing to the San Francisco 49ers, the last time in 1989 when Joe Montana brought the 49ers to victory, with defeat staring the team in the face in the last minute of play.

The team is streaky against the spread, with long runs of covering and failing. On Monday Night football they've been terrible against the spread.

CLEVELAND BROWNS

The Browns were formed right after the Second World War ended, in 1946, in a conference then known as the All-American Football Conference, the AAFC. Under Paul Brown they dominated the league, and when it was merged into the NFL, his Browns dominated that league as well. During those glory days, Otto Graham was their quarterback, one of the all-time great names at that position. But their crown jewel was the legendary Jim Brown, who came on board in 1956, and is considered the greatest runner in NFL history by many experts. Although they've won a bunch of NFL titles prior to the formation of the Super Bowl, the Browns have never won a Super Bowl, or even played in one.

Although they have a fine record against the spread on Monday Night games, they are generally a poor bet as favorites at home.

HOUSTON OILERS

This team goes back to 1960 in the old AFL, and both in 1960 and 1961 they won the title in that league with George Blanda, their quarterback, leading the way. Although the team has had individual stars such as Kenny Stabler, Earl Campbell and Warren Moon, they never seem to be able to get very far in the playoffs. They've been a disappointment to their fans year after year, beginning many seasons with high hopes and then fading away.

This is a tough team to bet on consistently, for they've had any number of years where they couldn't even reach a .500 mark against the spread.

PITTSBURGH STEELERS

Their first owner was Art Rooney, who is said to have bought the team at a racetrack one day, from some guy who wanted to unload it for small change. Of course, this was a long time ago. Rooney is now dead, but his family owns the team these days. They never made much of a stir in the old NFL, always an also-ran. Finally, in 1969, Chuck Noll became their coach, and after the first couple of dismal seasons, the team emerges as a winner. With stars such as Mean Joe Greene, Terry Bradshaw, Franco Harris, Jack Lambert and Jack Ham, they had a premier offense and defense and they truly were the team of the 1970s, winning four Super Bowls during that decade.

They have fallen down as a team and made little impact in the 1980s. They have been rebuilt and maybe one day when it all comes together again, they'll be a major force in the NFL.

Against Houston, they've had a number of low scoring games, and in the past, bettors have made some money betting this games as an Under game.

Western Division

DENVER BRONCOS

The Broncos came into the AFL in 1960, and for a decade and a half they struggled along, sometimes coming close against their main rivals, the old Oakland Raiders. In 1977, a new coach, Red Miller, came along and the "Orange Crush" was born. They went to the Super Bowl, and promptly lost to the Dallas Cowboys. Since then, they've hit the Super Bowl twice under quarterback John Elway, but lost in 1986 to the New York Giants, and in 1990, they were crushed, 55-10, by the San Francisco 49ers.

John Elway was known as the strongest arm in the NFL, but now the rap against him is that he can't win the big ones. Certainly the last humiliation in the Super Bowl is going to haunt the Broncos.

They play in Mile High Stadium, where the weather can turn treacherous in a hurry. Against San Diego, they've generally played low scoring games, and may be a good Under bet in this situation.

KANSAS CITY CHIEFS

The team originated in Dallas, where they were known as the Texans, but getting no support from the fans there, their owner, Lamar Hunt, moved them to Kansas City. Their first coach, Hank Stram, had one of the best football minds around, but he was fired in 1975. Since then, the team has struggled, occasionally making the playoffs, but not getting very far after that.

The Chiefs play at home on artificial turf in Arrowhead Stadium. Although they cover fairly well on Monday Night football, they've been known to have long losing streaks over the years against the spread.

LOS ANGELES RAIDERS

The Raiders were a mainstay in Oakland for many years, and certainly were one of the dominant teams in the NFL in the 1970s, with only Pittsburgh shining brighter. They won their first Super Bowl in 1976, and as a "wild card" entry won a Super Bowl in 1981 and again in 1983.

In 1982, the Raiders moved to Los Angeles and played in the Coliseum. They've been under the ownership of Al Davis for many years now, and it was always known as a superb organization. He paid the players top dollar and fostered an image of a renegade and dangerous group of men on the field.

With the move, and threats of another move to a different city or even back to Oakland, the team has suffered. One of the reasons, in addition to the transitory situation of the team, has been the lack of a first rate quarterback. Without a fine QB, the team has been floundering of late, and the once-mighty and proud Raiders became also-rans.

The team has performed well against the spread on Monday Night football, and in recent years have been known as a good Under bet.

SAN DIEGO CHARGERS

A mainstay of the old AFL, the Chargers have made some interesting runs at times, only to fall short. Twice they lost the AFL crown to the Oilers. In 1979, reaching the playoffs for the first time ever in the NFL, they lost in the first round again to the Oilers.

The team under Don Coryell, with the great Dan Fouts as QB, was able to rack up a lot of points in the 1980s, but it was strictly a passing show, with hardly any offense generated from the run. With a weak defense as well, the Chargers were vulnerable to good scoring teams.

In recent years, the Seattle Seahawks have had little trouble covering the spread against the Chargers. The Chargers also have had trouble as home favorites against the spread.

SEATTLE SEAHAWKS

This team came into the NFL as an expansion club in 1976, and have had a succession of good coaches, such as Chuck Knox and Jack Patera. They always seem on the verge of having a big year, only to disappoint the fans in the Emerald City.

They seem to do well covering at home against the spread, and as favorites. And on Monday Nights they have an outstanding record against the spread.

NATIONAL FOOTBALL CONFERENCE

This conference is made up generally of the older teams in the NFL, those that were playing ball twenty years before the birth of the American Football League. One of the On-line NFL teams, the team that dominated the 1970s, was the Pittsburgh Steelers, who moved to the AFC when the two leagues combined. In the 1970s, the stronger conference was the AFC; in the 1980s, the NFC became dominant.

Eastern Division

DALLAS COWBOYS

When the Dallas Cowboys came into being in 1960, its head coach was Tom Landry. He remained as coach through the 1988 season, when he was replaced by Jimmy Johnson, late of the Miami Hurricanes college team. A new owner had taken over the Cowboys, and Landry was given his walking papers quite unceremoniously.

Once "America's Team," the Dallas Cowboys now face an uncertain future. They're banking on young talent to get them through the 1990's, talent like Troy Aikman as QB. The team is in the middle of a rebuilding process, but it remains to be seen if a Jimmy Johnson can truly replace a Tom Landry, one of the finest and most innovative coaches the NFL ever had.

For a long time, with a couple of Super Bowl victories and players like Roger Staubach, "Too Tall" Jones, Drew Pearson, Charley Waters, Tony Dorsett and Randy White, the Cowboys caught the imaginations of America. They became a "national" team, with betting on them coming from all over the country. They were the Notre Dame of pro ball.

It's always been hard to make money betting on the Cowboys. Because of their fine teams and national attention, they were established favorites game after game, with bettors on them penalized by extra points. There was always plenty of action on Dallas. Now recently, they've been cast in the role underdogs, but even here they haven't covered well. This is a team that has to be studied carefully for the future before serious money can be bet on them.

NEW YORK GIANTS

This club dates its back to 1925, when it played at the Polo Grounds in New York City. In that year, the Chicago Bears came into town with the Galloping Ghost, the Iceman from Wheaton, Illinois, Red Grange, and the stands were filled to watch the Illinois star.

That's how the NFL was in those days, feast or famine, with a big star necessary to draw in the fans. It was catch as catch can as far as getting spectators to pay to see the games.

Over the years, the Giants were a great draw, with many fine teams and a number of NFL titles to their credit. Their big game in 1958, which they lost in overtime to the Baltimore Colts, led the way to the present popularity of the NFL brand of football. For that game, the Giants had players like Frank Gifford, Andy Robustelli, Roosevelt Brier and Sam Huff, truly a legendary team.

The 1970s were dismal for the Giants, but in the 1980s, they came alive again. In the 1986, it all came together for them as they crushed the Denver Broncos, 39-20 and became Super Bowl champions.

They play all their games in the Meadowlands of New Jersey at Giants Stadium, so their fans in New York have to travel out-of-state to watch them in person.

The Giants have always been known for their defensive powers, and are always a serious contender for an Under bet.

PHILADELPHIA EAGLES

The Eagles date back to 1933, but it took over a decade, to 1944, before they could be contenders for the NFL title. Finally in 1949 they won the title, and they repeated the next year against the LA Rams. In the 1950s, they were dormant as a contender, but in 1960 they added a third crown, led by the brilliant QB, Norm van Brocklin.

They've made it to the Super Bowl one time, in 1980 but they lost to the Oakland Raiders. They hired away Buddy Ryan from the Chicago Bears to be their coach in the late 1980s, and Ryan is known as a defensive genius. It remains to be seen if his skill will lift this team to the Super Bowl. For one thing, it plays in a tough division.

In recent years, the Eagles seem to shine as underdogs, but fail as favorites against the spread. With Ryan guiding them, they seem to be a good Under bet.

PHOENIX CARDINALS

In 1987, the Cardinals were taken away from St. Louis and moved to Phoenix. This was the second move for the club, which began life as the Chicago Cardinals and moved to St. Louis in 1960. For many years they weren't contenders, but then in 1974, led by Jim Hart's passing, Mel Gray's receiving and the brilliant running of Terry Metcalf, they won the Eastern Division title. They repeated the next year. However, both seasons ended with first round play-off losses.

There is no real joy in the move to Phoenix. The fans there haven't welcomed the team the way they were expected to, partly because they feel they've been gouged by the high prices charged to see a team that has played fairly mediocre ball since their transplantation to Arizonas sunny climes.

This team's stats have to be closely watched by bettors. With a whole new environment and new playing field, the old records may go out of the window. With lack of true fan support, the home field advantage may prove to be an illusory thing.

WASHINGTON REDSKINS

In 1937, the Redskins were moved from Boston to the nation's capital, where they have remained ever since. They now play in Robert F. Kennedy Stadium and have a loyal following among their fans there along the Potomac.

In their early days in the 1930's, the Redskins were blessed with Sammy Baugh, whom many consider the greatest quarterback who ever played the game. Not only was he possessed of a magnificent arm, but he held punting records and was an outstanding safety for the Redskins.

However, despite his prowess on the field, they were demolished in 1940 by the Chicago Bears led by Sid Luckman, 73-0, the most one-sided title game ever in the NFL. It was the old single wing of the Redskins against the new T formation of the Bears. After that game, the T formation was the formation used in the NFL, and it still is intact today.

In 1942, the Redskins won an NFL title, but though they were in the title game in 1943 and 1945, during the war years, they couldn't manage wins. With a stingy boos, George Marshall, the team slowly sank in the 1950s. It revived for a moment under Vince Lombardi, but after his demise from cancer, it wasn't until George Allen became coach of the team in 1971 that they became a factor again. He traded away draft rights for players now, and reached the Super Bowl, only to lose to Miami, 14-7, in 1972.

In 1982 they revenged that loss by beating Miami 27-17 in the Super Bowl, behind the leadership of Joe Theismann, their QB. That was their last Super Bowl victory.

Over the years, they've done fairly well as a favorite against the spread. The New York Giants seem to give them a lot of trouble, and they've failed against their division rivals recently.

Central Division

CHICAGO BEARS

The "Monsters of the Midway," as this team was called from many years, was the inspired child of George Halas, who, more than any other individual, was responsible for the birth and sustenance of the NFL. The original Bears were moved from Decatur, Illinois, by Halas, and he was their first coach in Chicago.

In 1922, the NFL began its career as a football league, and one of the showpieces was the Bears. Halas introduced Red Grange to pro football, and under his stardom, the team drew great crowds. It made money and the league kept going.

It wasn't until 1932 that the Bears won their first NFL title.

Their backfield that year had both Red Grange and Bronco Nagurski, two of the greatest players ever to handle the pigskin.

A great coach, Clark Shaughnessy introduced the T formation to the team, and in 1939 he got Sid Luckman right out of Columbia to run it. Their 1940 title game win over the Redskins, 73-0, shocked the NFL, and everyone ran to the T formation.

They won again in 1941, beating the New York Giants, 37-9. After the war was over, Halas again became their coach, and again, in 1946, they won an NFL title. Then, as quick as a wink, they started fading. They weren't much of a factor all during the 1950s, and in the 1960, despite having players of the caliber of Gale Sayers and Dick Butkus, Halas couldn't win a title for the Bears.

He left coaching in 1967.

After a number of mediocre years, the Bears got on track in 1984, going to the Super Bowl, where they lost to San Francisco, 23-0, but in 1985, with Jim McMahon as their quarterback, they prevailed, 46-10 over New England and finally became Super Bowl champs.

Now George Halas has passed away, but the family still runs the organization, trying to keep the fine tradition of the Monsters of the Midway.

DETROIT LIONS

In 1934 they came into being, and by the second season of play they were NFL champions. Among their stars were Dutch Clark, and the spectacular Whizzer White, who eventually became a Supreme Court Justice.

After the Second World War they were mediocre, but with the acquisition of Bobby Layne, they were once more champions of the NFL in 1952. They were in other title games but in 1957, underdogs most of the season, they went on to crush the Cleveland Browns for the title, 59-14.

The team struggled from that year on. Occasionally they've gotten into the playoffs, but have never played in the Super Bowl. Their games are played in a domed stadium in Pontiac, Michigan.

The Lions play in a very tough division, knows as the "Black and Blue" division, and that has made their seasons even more difficult.

GREEN BAY PACKERS

The "Pack" were named after the Indian Packing Company of Green Bay, and they're the oldest of all the original NFL teams, beginning their life as a pro club way back in 1919.

It took over a decade before they really made their mark, then they won three straight NFL titles in 1929, 1930 and 1931. During the 1930s and 1940s, they had a tremendous rivalry with the Chicago Bears. The key player on the Packers at that time was Don Hutson, who many consider the greatest end who ever played in the NFL.

The team was submerged in the standing until Vince Lombardi took over in the late 1950s, and guided the team to a dominant position in the 1960s. They won an NFL title in 1961, with stars such as Ray Nitschke, Forrest Gregg, Jim Ringo, Jim Taylor, Paul Hornung and Bart Starr, They won the first two Super Bowls ever played, and the Packers became the darlings of the media and were nationally followed as America's favorite team.

In 1969, Lombardi retired, and from then on it was downhill for the Pack. They sank to the cellar in their division by 1970, and never again reached the

Super Bowl. At times they've shown some luster, and excited their fans all over again, but the rap against the club is the small-town atmosphere of Green Bay, with a lot of racial problems between the players and the locals.

MINNESOTA VIKINGS

In 1961, as an expansion team, the Vikings came into the NFL. In 1967, they hired a new coach, Bud Grant, who became a mainstay for decades, and under his guidance, the Vikings went to four Super Bowls. However, they never won one of those games, and they were knows as a team that couldn't win the Big One.

Their most famous quarterback was the scrambler, Fran Tarkenton, who holds a host of NFL passing records. Known at one time as the "Purple People Eaters" the Vikings featured an impressive defense.

They've made a few runs in the playoffs since their Super Bowl defeats, and they have a good organization behind them, and should be a factor for years to come.

They play their home games at the Metrodome, and thus the bitter weather that features Minnesota winters in not a factor in their games.

TAMPA BAY BUCCANEERS

In 1976 Tampa Bay was given a franchise in the NFL as an expansion team, and their first coach was John McKay, formerly of USC.

They started off losing 26 games in a row, and it wasn't until December 11, 1977 that they finally won a game, beating New Orleans. By 1979, with Ricky Bell, their fine runner leading the way, they made the playoffs. Although they made the playoffs a couple of more times, their coach, John McKay, resigned after the 1984 season, and that same year, Ricky Bell tragically died.

The team got worse after that. Desperate for a quality quarterback, they drafted Vince Testaverde of Miami University after the 1986 season and they've pinned their hopes on his strong arm.

In their own division games, they've been terrible against the spread, a factor to watch for.

Western Division

ATLANTA FALCONS

The Falcons were an expansion team in the NFL, beginning their existence in 1966. When the two leagues merged in 1970, for some strange reason, they were shoved into the Western Division. Perhaps there will be a re-alignment sometime in the future.

After foundering around for years, they finally made the playoffs in 1978, then fell apart in 1979, and in a complete turnaround, as "Falcon Fever" raged through Atlanta, won their division's title in 1980. They lost early in the playoffs, and after that, except for 1982 they haven't even made the playoffs.

The main rap against the club is the ownership. Ted Turner, who seems to own everything in Atlanta, doesn't really know much about football, and the people he's hired to run the club haven't been able to get the kind of personnel necessary to make this team a contender.

They've had trouble covering at home, perhaps due to a lack of fan support.

LOS ANGELES RAMS

The team was moved from Cleveland to Los Angeles in 1945, and the owner, Dan Reeves, had the foresight to realize that Southern California would be a haven for a pro football team, with glorious weather and a burgeoning population.

Despite some outstanding teams, led by Bob Waterfield, their QB, it wasn't until 1951 that they won their first NFL title, with another quarterback, Norm Van Brocklin, backing up Waterfield.

The early 1960s saw a team loaded with talented personnel but not going anywhere until 1966 when George Allen took over as coach. He guided them to the playoffs, as did other coaches who followed. They'd win their division title, but lose somewhere in the playoff rounds, not quite making it to the SuperBowl.

Then, in 1979, the year they moved out of LA to Anaheim, they got to the Super Bowl, losing to Pittsburgh.

After John Robinson took over as coach in 1983, the team played consistently good ball, but the rap here is that the Rams have been too conservative a club on offense, never able to win that Super Bowl. In playoffs they've generally had low scoring teams, relying on bread and butter plays rather than a daring offensive scheme.

The franchise has loyal fans and money behind it and it tries hard year after year. Perhaps some innovation is the form of a creative coach is all they need to go all the way.

NEW ORLEANS SAINTS
In 1967, the Saints were taken into the NFL as an expansion team, and put in the Western Division with the merger of the two leagues. Another crazy place for a team rooted in the South.

The team was terrible from the start, and a succession of good coaches, such as Hank Stram couldn't get them going anywhere.

Having had all those bad years, leading up to the end of the 1980 decade, the team has been improving as the 1990s unfold. They have improved the quality of their personnel and play tremendously, and had, in Morten Andersen, their placekicker, the best in the NFL.

No longer a patsy for the other clubs and especially those in their division, the Saints give battle these days, and seem to be improving year by year.

SAN FRANCISCO 49ers
The 49ers came into existence at the end of World War II, in the old All-American Football Conference. They had some good stars

in the 1940s and 1950s, men like QB Frankie Albert, and fine runners such as Hugh McElhenny and Joe Perry.

There were decades of frustration for the 49er fans, until they won their division crown in 1970, only to lose the NFC title to the Dallas Cowboys. It wasn't until Bill Walsh took over as coach in 1978 that things started to happen for the Bay Area team.

Walsh was a brilliant football man, innovative, with a fine feel for picking solid draft choices. By 1983, led by Joe Montana, they made the playoffs, and in 1984, won the first of their Super Bowls over Miami, 38-16. By the end of the 1980s, they were the dominant team in the NFL, and their brilliant victories over Cincinnati and Denver established them as the team of the 1980s.

Walsh has resigned as coach with little change in their strength. They have a fine organization behind them, paying the biggest salaries in the NFL. And in Joe Montana, they have had one of the finest QBs in NFL history, and perhaps the best clutch QB of all time.

4. BOXING

A. INTRODUCTION

Big-time boxing depends more and more on charismatic person-alities, and the public's interest in those personalities. A Muham-med Ali or Mike Tyson can transform a drab heavyweight division into an exciting one. When Larry Holmes or the Spinks brothers were champions, the public yawned and took little interest, and that included the betting public.

Other divisions fare the same way. Michael Nunn is a dull fighter, while Sugar Ray Leonard is an exciting showman. When the fight involves one of these charismatic personalities up against a good fighter, there's a lot of betting action. When two dullards are fight-ing, the bookies get little action.

An ideal fight for the bookies is one where one of the beloved personalities is literally fighting for his boxing life, as in the Larry Holmes-Ali fight. The action was hot and heavy, that is, the betting action. It finally settled at 8-5 in favor of Holmes, though experts in the know thought the fight should have been 6-1 or higher in favor of Holmes.

However, the boxing money line, like all other sports betting lines, is affected by the public's perception of the event, not by the relative talents of the men involved. Ali was a legend and had given the boxing fans many great moments over the years. Holmes was colorless and generally disliked. Money poured in on Ali when logic dictated that it should go on Holmes. It was a one-sided fight, with Holmes winning easily by a TKO when Ali couldn't answer the bell for the eighth round.

B. THE BOXING BETTING LINE

Boxing is similar to baseball in that there's a money line, and no point spread. Whereas baseball's standard money line is the 20¢ one, in boxing, it's a 40¢ line.

40¢ or 2 Point Line

Quote	True Odds	Bookmaker's Edge Underdog	Bookmaker's Edge Favorite
"6-5 Pick"	1-1	8.33	8.33
5-7	6-5	9.09	6.49
6-8	7-5	8.33	5.21
7-9	8-5	7.69	4.27
8-10	9-5	7.14	3.57
9-11	2-1	6.67	3.03
10-12	11-5	6.25	2.60
11-13	12-5	5.88	2.26
12-14	13-5	5.56	1.98
13-15	14-5	5.26	1.75
14-18	16-5	9.52	2.65
15-20	7-2	11.11	2.78

First, we should note that the bookie's vig is quite high in the 40¢ line. Instead of a "pick-em" bet where the gambler lays 11-10, with the 40¢ or "2-point" line, he must lay 6-5, giving the bookie an edge of 8.33%.

This edge is very difficult to overcome in the long run, and it's why there's not that much action on boxing events. An 8-5 wager, which we quoted before when discussing Ali and Holmes, would be a 6-8 quote. All quotes are to $5.

By 6-8, we mean that the favorite is 8-5, the second number, while the underdog is 6-5, the first number.

Here's how it works.

If you bet on the underdog Ali, you'd only get $6 for your $5 bet. You can see that betting on Ali you'd give the bookmaker an 833% edge, while betting on Holmes, it's down to 5.21%.

The reason the line is called a 40¢ one, is because of the differential between the quotes.

> 8-5 equals 1.60 - 1.00
> 6-5 equals 1.20 - 1.00

The difference is 40¢.

Bookmakers don't put up quotes on all fights, only those where action can come in on both sides; otherwise they're doing the gambling. That's why we mentioned the fighters in the public's eye, and how important they are to bookies.

When a fighter is so much better than his opponent we get lines of 5-1 or even 10-1 and beyond. This was the case with Mike Tyson and his early string of hapless opponents. In those situations, the quote would be for example, "10-1 and out," which means that no betting is permitted on the favorite. The bookie would only take action on the underdog.

Well, the bookies made a fortune fight after fight, until the Buster Douglas battle, when a man quoted as 20-1 underdog by some bookmakers demolished Tyson.

Because of the nature of boxing, which had been controlled for many years by organized crime, with "Mr. Gray," Frankie Carbo, running much of it for the mob, many fights today are suspect, even though mob influence has waned tremendously. After all, if a fighter goes "into the tank" and loses intentionally, how can it be proved?

Bookmakers get leery when a fight suddenly brings a lot of action to one side. In those cases, the fight is quickly *taken off the boards* , that is , no more action is allowed.

This sudden influx of money doesn't mean there's a "fix" involved. It may mean that gamblers know something - perhaps the fighter isn't feeling well or has been training poorly, or has big emotional problems.

But once the money pours in, and the bookmaker feels he's getting "sided", it goes off the boards.

C. THE HAZARDS OF PRIZEFIGHT BETTING

Today boxing is an international sport, with many fighters coming from Central and South America and the Caribbean, especially in the lighter weight classes. A fighter from the Dominican Republic fighting at home will get "hometown officiating" and is going to have to be knocked out in order for the opponent to win. Anything remotely close will go to the hometown boy.

This happens when a favorite son fights an opponent anywhere. Usually three judges mark a fight, and see the same bout, and yet they may radically differ. Bettors worry about a fix being in with the judges. There are boxing commissions all over the place, and three championship groups, the WBA, WBC and IBF.

Everything is complicated and upside down in boxing. Nothing is simple, and therefore it's suspect.

I've watched fights where it was a certainty that one boxer won, and yet the other would get the decision. A fighter could be battered, knocked down, and have one eye closed by the other boxer, who was unscathed, and yet the decision went to the battered fighter, unanimously.

Even on big fights on national TV. After years of this, the public has lost confidence in the sanctity of boxing, and many feel its a crooked and brutal sport not fit for a civilized society.

If you're going to watch a fight, and see your fighter win easily, and find that the judges scored it the other way, what can you do? Nothing, except stop betting on fights. And that's what has been happening more and more.

The boxing betting business is dying, and with good reason. Every now and then it resurrects itself with a big fight, but those fights are generally manufactured in hype. And how many times can Sugar Ray Leonard retire and un-retire, and be shoved in against Hearns or Duran who also makes a comeback just for this one fight?

It becomes a joke to the American public. They get sucked in time and time again, only to watch some dismal match by overage fighters whose skill left them years before.

So, one of the main hazards involved with betting on boxing matches is that the result won't be fairly determined by the judges. Or that you'll be sucked in by the hype and bet on a fighter who couldn't fight his way through a bag of potato chips.

We'll assume that by this time you're going to think logically before making any kind of bet, so when in doubt about a the officiating or any other aspect of the bout, simply pass on the fight. Don't bet it. Otherwise, not only will you end up getting aggravated, but you'll lose money as well.

Be very careful betting on boxing. You're giving away a lot in terms of the vig, and you can't be sure of the result, even if your fighter seemed to win the match.

D. WINNING STRATEGIES

The only viable matches to bet on are those where the line permits you t bet on either boxer. In other words, if the fight is 8-1 and out, and you can only bet on some bum who doesn't stand a chance, that's no choice at all.

Occasionally one of these long shots such as Buster Douglas, will come through. Practically all of the time they're sitting ducks, "opponents" in the terminology of boxing, mere setups to make the favorite's record look good.

When the fighters come into the ring with a money quote allowing you to go either way, then there are some things you should look for so that you make an intelligent wager.

1. If a young fighter has been moved up slowly, with a fine or even unbeaten record, and is matched against a name fighter who is over-the-hill, the young fighter is probably ready to win the fight.

The aging fighter has had his day and is no longer a moneymaker. The youngster is ready for the big money. The handlers aren't usually going to forfeit the big money   they are pretty sure their fighter can win. Go with the young fighter.

2. If a young fighter is going at a longer distance but the rap against him is that he's never gone that distance, don't worry.

If he has good trainers, they'll prepare him physically for the new distance. It also may be that he's been knocking out fighters in early rounds. That shouldn't worry you - this longer distance. Go with the young fighter superbly trained, and moving up.

3. If an aging fighter is trying for a comeback, and has beaten a few weaklings, and is now up against a strong name fighter who's younger, go with the youngster.

Especially if he's well handled. I've seen comebacks come to a quick end time and time again, with one bad beating finally putting the formerly fine fighter back to permanent retirement.

4. If a former champion is again fighting after a layoff, the chances are he'll be matched up against a series of weak opponents.

If you can get bets down on the former champion against these pushovers, by all means make the bets. A good example is the comeback of George Foreman, ten years after he retired.

But if this same former champion now must face a younger champion, then the hype is over, and the former champion is a bad bet. Forget about nostalgia in the ring - it's a hard brutal business, and age punishes fighters more than any other athletes.

5. If a fighter of quality has retired and come back for a big payday immediately against a fighter who's active, go against the retired fighter.

People could have made a lot of money betting against Gerry Cooney, everytime he made a "comeback" for a big purse, and ended up on his back. And if he comes back again, the media hype will once more tune up and make him a viable contestant. Don't believe it. This "white hype" will lose your money every time he climbs into the ring.

6. When a slugger meets a slugger, with both men in their prime, I always like the stronger hitter.

It'll be a wide-open fight, and the stronger punches will invariably tell.

7. When a boxer meets a boxer, I look to the cleverer and better boxer. He should win.

If you can't tell who's better, stay away from betting on the fight. But if you know one is superior to the other, and you can get a bet down on the better boxer, do so.

8. The most interesting matchups come when both men can box, but one can box and slug at the same time.

That was the Billy Conn-Joe Louis first fight. If the boxer sticks to his routine, he has a chance, but many of them decide to show they can hit also, and ends up going to sleep.

Or, what happens is that the slugger doesn't even give the boxer the chance to set up; he simply knocks him out quickly. The second Louis-Schmeling fight; the Tyson-Spinks fight are good examples of this. When a fighter is an awesome slugger, there aren't any boxers going to keep up with him.

The exceptions come when age plays a role. Thus Dempsey was too old for Tunney and lost to him. Look at the fighter moving up and the one moving down. It happens time and time again in boxing. Rarely do two great fighter both meet in their prime, with both in the ascendancy. Go with the up-and-coming fighter in these matchups and you won't go wrong.

9. Don't get nostalgic about fighters or go against logic.

Don't remember the old great fighter and think the shell now stepping in the ring is the same man with the same abilities. That was the Louis-Marciano and Ali-Holmes fights, pitiful affairs to those who loved those great champions.

10. Shop for value when betting on prize fights.

The line may change form bookie to bookie. The bookie has a big edge and it make a big difference to you if you lay 7-5 instead of 8-5, or get 5-2 instead 2-1. Shop around. If you can't get what you consider a fair price, don't bet the fight.

With these principles in mind, you should be able to approach boxing as a money-making vehicle for your bets.

5. BASEBALL

When we refer to baseball betting, we're only going to discuss Major-League baseball. College games aren't bet on, nor is there a line developed for these games. It's the teams in the *show* that get the attention of the gamblers.

Unlike football or basketball, in which there's a pointspread, with one team ranked so many points above another, in baseball we have what is known as a **money line**.

With a money line, in order to win your bet, your team must win the game straight-up. It doesn't matter what the final score is, as long as your team wins.

For example, if you bet on the Yankees against the White Sox, and the final score is Yankees 1 White Sox 0, you have won. If the White Sox squeaked in a winner by that identical score, you lost. Simple as that. So remember, you need winners and lots of them to beat the bookie in baseball.

Under and over bets are also permitted, but these are made at the usual 11-10 vig that we've seen before in football betting, with the bookie having the best of it by 4.54%.

A. THE MONEY LINE

Many people don't bet on baseball games because they can't figure out the line, and what it means. But it's not that difficult to comprehend. So let's go over it step by step.

Let's assume that the Oakland As are playing the White Sox at Oakland Coliseum. The As are the favorites for this particular game. Let's assume the line reads as follows:

OAKLAND White Sox 6 1/2 -7 1/2

The As are at home, thus they're capitalized. They're also favorites and thus listed first. What does 6 1/2 -7 1/2 mean?

These numbers relate to a theoretical $5 bet, with the lower number always quoted first and relating to the underdog.

If you bet on the A's , who are the favorites, you must lay $7.50 (7 1/2) to win $5 and if you bet on the White Sox, you're only receiving $6,50 (6 1/2) for your $5 bet. Usually, in betting casinos, the same line may be quoted as follows:

OAKLAND White Sox +130 -150 or +$1.30 - $1.50

This is the same as 6 1/2 -7 1/2, except that they've been doubled to reflect a line based on a theoretical $1 bet. If you bet on Oakland, you've got to lay $1.50 to win $1.00, and if you bet that same $1.00 on the White Sox, you're only getting $1.30 if you win.

You can see where the bookie makes his money from this line. Between the two figures of $1.30 and $1.50 there's a 20¢ gap. In fact, this is the standard 20¢ line you'll be betting into if you wager on baseball games.

The correct odds on the game is somewhere in between, right in the middle. If the bookie gave you $1.40-1.00 whether or not you bet on Oakland or the White Six, he'd have no edge whatsoever. But he ends up with the 20 cent line penalizing both bettors.

One has to lay more than the 1.40 (1.50) when betting on the favorite, the Oakland in this case, and the other only gets 1.30 instead of the 1.40 when betting on the underdog White Sox.

Looking at the following table, we can see the Bookie's edge on this very bet. If you bet on the favorite, you're giving the bookie 2.78%, and if you wager on the underdog, it's costing you 4.17% in vig of 4.55%.

20¢ or 1 Point Line

Quote	True Odds	Bookmaker's % Edge Underdog	Favorite
11-10	1-1	4.55	4.55
5-6	11-10	4.76	3.97
5 1/2-6 1/2	6-5	4.55	3.50
6-7	13-10	4.35	3.11
6 1/2- 7 1/2	7-5	4.17	2.78
7-8	3-2	4.00	2.50
7 1/2-8 1/2	8-5	3.85	2.26
8-9	17-10	3.70	2.06
8 1/2-9 1/2	9-5	3.57	1.88
9-10	19-10	3.45	1.72
9 1/2-10 1/2	2-1	3.33	1.59
10-11	21-10	3.23	1.47
10 1/2-11 1/2	11-5	3.13	1.36
11-12	23-10	3.03	1.26
11 1/2-12 1/2	12-5	2.94	1.18
12-13	5-2	2.86	1.10
12 1/2-13 1/2	13-5	2.78	1.03

Looking at the line, we see clearly that the bookie's edge is less when you bet the favorite, except in the 11-10 situation, when either side pays 4.54%.

Does this mean that it pay always to bet on the favorite?

Not necessarily.

Let's look at the next table.

The Payoff Chart

The Vegas Line	Take Odds	$1.00 Payoff
+220	11-5	2.20
+200	2-1	2.00
+180	9-5	1.80
+170	8 1/2-5	1.70
+160	8-5	1.60
+150	7 1/2-5	1.50
+140	7-5	1.40
+130	6 1/2-5	1.30
+120	6-5	1.20
+110	5 1/2-5	1.10
Even	1-1	1.00
-110	5-5 1/2	.91
-120	5-6	.83
-130	5- 6 1/2	.77
-140	5-7	.71
-150	5- 7 1/2	.67
-160	5-8	.62
-170	5-8 1/2	.59
-180	5-9	.55
-200	1-2	.50
-220	5-11	.45
-240	5-12	.42
-260	5-13	.38
-280	5-14	.36
-300	1-3	.33

Two other notations may be seen:
"No Rating Given"
"Pick' Em" or "Even"

On this table, we see the profit you make every time you wager $1.00. A Vegas Line of +220, means that you've bet $1.00 to win $2.20. Let's go back to our Oakland-White Sox game, where the line reads +130 - 150.

If we bet on the favorite, we'd have to lay $1.50 to win $1.00. If we look at the column Profit to $1.00, we see that we'd win only 67¢ for every dollar bet. If we bet on the dog, the White Sox, we'd get $1.30 for every dollar bet, for a profit of $1.30.

Betting on the underdog, and laying $1.50 forces us to win 60% of the time just to break even. The next table shows us the break even point for all bets in which we're laying odds as the favorite bettor.

Break-Even Point		
Line	Odds	Pct.
-1.10	5-5 1/2	53%
-1.20	5-6	55%
-1.30	5- 6 1/2	57%
-1.40	5-7	58%
-1.50	5-8	60%
-1.60	5-8 1/2	62%
-1.70	5-8 1/2	63%
-1.80	5-9	64%
-2.00	1-2	67%
-2.20	5-11	69%
-2.40	5-12	71%

Here's how the table works.

Let's say that we have made 100 $1.00 bets laying 1.50-1 on the favorite. If we break it down, it looks like this, assuming 60 wins and 40 losses.

| 60 wins | +$60 |
| 40 losses | -$60 (40 x $1.50) |

There's no gain and no loss. We've broken even exactly. To win 60% of the time is a major effort. A big-league team, to do this in a 162 game schedule, must win 97 games. So, even though the bookie's edge is lower when we bet on favorites, we can see that a steady diet of underdog wins on our part should really pay off.

Let's assume that we have only bet the underdog at that same 6 1/2 -7 1/2. We won't win as many times, but if we win 44% of the time, and lose 56% of the time, we'll still turn a slight profit. Here's how this works:

44 wins (x.130)	+$57.20
56 losses	-$56.00
Net Win	**+$1.20**

If we bet the favorite at 1.70, laying that to $1, we have to win 63% of the time.

63 wins	+$63.00
37 losses (x$1.70)	- $62.90
Net Win	**+ $ .10**

Or just about even.

But again, let's translate that into something you baseball fans can understand. For any team to win 63% of the time, it would have to win over 102 games per season, and just how many clubs are going to be able to do that for you?

The next table is a more exact rendition of just what percentage of games you must win at various quotes on the money line.

128

Break-Even Point Against the Line

Underdog		Favorite	
	Percentage Needed		Percentage Need
The Line	To Win	The Line	To Win
110 Pick	52.4	110 Pick	52.4
Even	50.0	-120	54.6
+110	47.6	-130	56.5
+120	45.5	-140	58.5
+130	43.5	-150	60.2
+140	41.7	-160	61.7
+150	40.0	-170	62.9
+160	38.5	-180	64.5
+170	37.0	-200	66.7
+180	35.7	-220	69.0
+200	33.3	-240	70.4
+220	31.3	-260	72.5
+240	29.4	-280	73.5

A final word on the money line. There are others, ranging up to 40¢, but you don't want to bet them. If you're a really high roller, you may be able to get a 15¢ line (the difference between the favorite and the underdog expressed as 15¢ rather than 20¢).

If you can get that line, you've cut the bookie's edge, but don't count on being offered a 15¢ line unless you're betting really big bucks.

Remember, to beat the line, you've got to beat the price. Forget about winning 53% of the time, as in football or basketball betting. You've got to beat the price consistently. To do this, you've got to win games.

B. WINNING STRATEGIES

PITCHERS AND THE LINE

When any line is put out, the pitchers for that game are named and that's what basically determines the line. A great pitcher can limit the number of runs a team can score against him almost single-handedly.

If a team can't score enough runs, it can't win the game. That's why pitching is more important than team strength, which is also a factor, but not as great as pitching.

Some experts say pitching is 80% of the game, others 70%, still others abut 65%. Whatever the figure, pitching predominates in baseball. A team can't win without those good arms going for them.

However, I'd like to add this to the discussion. Are the starting pitchers 70% of the game, or 80% of the game? Not at all. They count a great deal, but now teams are structured in a different manner than 30 years ago, for example, when a pitcher's completed games were important.

Today, the starting pitcher doesn't have the same relative strength that he used to have. He's not expected to go all the way. And if he runs into trouble, he can easily be yanked out of there.

A strong team not only has five starters going in rotation, but a middle reliever able to go about four or five innings, a setup, or short man able to go a couple of innings, and a closer, who can shut off a team's run production for one inning.

You must take this fact into account when betting on a team to win a game. How strong is the bullpen? If the bullpen is powerful, and has the long and short reliever and the closer of high caliber, then your chances of winning your bet are greatly enhanced. The opposing team is going to be facing strength all the way. Its run production is going to be crippled by great arms.

What also hurts batters is a new pitcher coming in the game. Just when they've adjusted to the speed and delivery of the starter, here comes someone new out of the bullpen. And in the last inning or two, if the game is on the line, here comes the star of the team, the pitcher with the great pitch, the man who can squelch any fire erupting from the bats of the opposition.

The relievers are measured not so much in wins and losses but in saves. A team loaded with pitchers with a lot of saves is a team you can confidently bet on. If they get ahead, this team can hold a lead. The teams that have weak relievers blow leads and just when you're sitting back about to enjoy a win, you suddenly see that their starter has been knocked out, and some reliever is giving up five runs to drown your bet.

Here are various factors that you must study in order to make an intelligent choice about a bet. All of these factors relate to pitchers.

1. Study the won-loss record of the pitcher, and his ERA (earned run average).

A brilliant won-loss record, of say 4-1, may be pretty meaningless if the pitcher has an ERA of 5.64. It may be that his team has been pounding in runs and supporting him with at least six per game. But what about this game, when the opposing pitcher has an ERA of 3.10?

The ERA is the most important stat you can have on a pitcher. It tells about his performance in a way no other stat can.

2. Don't study pitcher against pitcher. Study pitcher against lineup.

If, in the previous example, we'll expect the 4-1 pitcher with the big ERA to give up five runs against the other team, while the other pitcher, with an ERA of a little over 3.00 will give up only 3 runs, then we should have the win in the column of the pitcher with the lower ERA.

How do we know what a pitcher will do against a particular team? Look at the stats again. Baseball is a game loaded with statistics. You can find anything you want. Check out *The Sporting News*, which you should have as your bible if you're betting seriously on baseball.

There are a ton of books listed for all kinds of baseball stats, and off-beat stats, and various ways to analyze them. These books come and go, and some may be out of date. My suggestion is to contact the *Gambler's Book Club*, 630 So. 11th Street, Las Vegas, NV 89101, 1-800 634-6243, to get a catalogue of their baseball books, or to order them. They're absolutely the best source for anything on gambling.

3. Study the normal rotation of each pitcher, and see how he does in that rotation, and how well or poorly he performs when pitching out of rotation.

Some managers care only about wins at all costs and will destroy their pitchers to get that. But fine pitchers are like thoroughbreds. They'll come through for you, but you must pamper them. They're fragile. You hurt their pitching arm, and you have a useless athlete. You have a horse with a broken leg.

If a pitcher is pushed to throw too often during the early part of the season, his fatigued arm will catch up with him sooner or later. Follow the teams that have little regard for their pitching staff, who push for early season wins at all costs. These are the teams that will fall apart late in the season.

4. Look at the no-decision games.

We know, of course, that all pitching efforts don't end up with a **W** or an **L**. Many are no-decisions, where a reliever picks up the win or the loss. Study these games, and see how many were won with the pitcher who's starting today. This is an important stat that is often overlooked, with bettors blindly studying the won-loss records.

For example, suppose a pitcher has a 3-2 won-lost record, but there are three games in which he started where there was no decision involving him one way or the other. Of those three games, his team won 2 and lost 1.

Now we have an interesting stat. If we had bet on this pitcher, we'd have won 5 games and lost 3, for a 62.5% win ratio. That should make us money.

Let's look at another pitcher. His record is also 3-2, but in the three games he started that he didn't get the decision, his team lost 2 and won 1. Now we have a record of 4-4 for all the games this pitcher started, a mere 50%. We've got to lose with that stat unless his team was the dog most of the time.

But with his won-lost record of 3-2, his team may be the favorite at 1.30-1 and we're not getting value betting on his arm.

5. Whether a pitcher won, lost or had no decision, if he's been pitching well lately, then he's worth a hard look.

Pitchers round into shape and get very sharp for a period of time. That's when we want to get on them. If we see that pitcher A had pitched eight innings the last time out, allowed one run, but had no decision, we know he's annoyed that he didn't get a big W, and this time out, he'll be sharp and go for the missing win. He may be worth a big bet.

Conversely, avoid pitchers who have been struggling lately, or better yet, go against them. You may not know the reason for their current problems, but you don't have to know this. All you have to know is that they're not pitching well. Maybe they have a sore elbow, maybe they have drug problems, maybe marital problems. Whatever the reason, don't get your money involved, except to go against them.

6. Look at the stats of pitchers against particular teams.

Some pitchers have the hex on a team for some reason or another. This trend should be bet on till it is broken. If you have a hunch, that's not enough. Respect trends, and don't go against them.

Conversely, some pitchers just can't win against certain teams. Again, respect this trend, and if you don't have to lay more than 1.60, go with it.

7. No matter how fine the pitcher is, try and avoid any situation where you have to lay 1.70 or more.

That win ratio of 63% to just break even is a powerful wall put up against increasing your bankroll. Look for other spots. There are plenty of games played every day, enough for you to find a better place for your money.

8. Good value for your money may be there when a rookie is pitching for the first few times in the majors.

The bookies don't really have a line on him, and if he's going against an experienced pitcher, he may be the dog. These may be good spots for your money, especially if you can get +1.30 and up for your wager. After all, this guy is a major leaguer. He must have something. The bookie is making a decision that he's weak, but the manager has put him on his staff. Who knows best? In this situation, if I respect the manager, I go with him, and bet on his pitcher. I'm getting good value here.

With rookies, you may be getting value for a long time, through several starts, before the oddsmakers wake up to the fact that this kid can win games. Meanwhile, you've cashed in some good winning bets.

STATISTICS TO CONSIDER

So far, we've discussed pitching as a key element in picking winners. But other factors certainly have to be studied. The more we know, the better our chance of winning, if we put the knowledge to logical use.

1. Won-Lost records of individual teams.

These must be studied so that we avoid teams that win so few of their games, that no matter what the money price, we'll end up losing money. We want not only to narrow our losing percentage; we want to increase our winning percentage, get those wins on our side and cash the bets. Then everything takes care of itself.

As the season progresses, study the won-lost records of the teams in both leagues. Look for the winning teams, and follow their trends. I'd rather, in some instances, have a winning team with a mediocre pitcher, than a losing team with a good pitcher. The losing team generally finds a way to lose the game. The winning team finds a way to win.

2. One of the stats shown in most papers, along with the won-lost record of the individual teams, is the present streak of won or lost games.

The following table show an example of this:

	W	L	Pct.	GB	L10	Str.
Milwaukee	21	14	.600	-	5-5	L1
Boston	20	16	.556	2	6-4	W1
Toronto	21	19	.525	3	4-6	L1
Cleveland	19	18	.514	3 1/2	5-5	L2
Detroit	18	22	.450	6	7-3	W7
Baltimore	16	22	.421	7	4-6	L1
New York	14	21	.400	7 1/2	4-6	L2

W = Win, **L** = Loss, **Pct.**= Winning Percentage, **GB** = Games Behind First Place, **L10** = Record for Last 10 Games, **Streak** = Games won or lost in succession.

If a team has won or lost less than three games, I'd discount this for any streak. However, once the team has won at least three games in a row, we have a situation that has to be looked into carefully.

The best chances of a team continuing the streak is at home. However, the price may become prohibitive, often above 2.00-1. We can't afford to go that high on any game, for if we lose, we have to win too many games just to catch up with that one loss.

We want to get in bets for less than 1.70-1, to avoid needing 63% wins just to break even. With these streaks, we look for a home game at a price below 1.70. Those are our best bets and will win the most money for us.

On the road, the odds might be not that tough. A team on a streak may very well be below 1.70, coming in at 1.40, for example. These are the games to bet when a team is on a streak.

3. Go against the team on a three game losing streak.

Our best play here is if the team is on the road, for the best chances of the losing streak continuing is away from home. Again, we have to watch the price, for we want to stay at 1.60 or below. Sometimes, despite the losing streak, the bookies will make this team the favorite. That's our best shot. We may be betting against a superior pitcher, but the team may not support the pitcher. The team may have a losing psychology.

We have a lot going for us whenever we lay a small price betting against the team with a long losing streak. But we have even more going for us, if we can end up betting on the underdog in this situation. That's real value that will make a lot of money for us.

4. Careful consideration must be given to teams that are underdogs when playing at home.

They won't win more than about 48% of the time, but any price of 1.10 or better will make money for us. Having already seen that we want to avoid teams with losing steaks of three or more, if we eliminate these, and concentrate on other home dogs, we can find some good spots for our money.

In the early pat of the season, before the strengths of the various teams has been sorted out by the oddsmakers, we'll find a number of good situations, where the home dogs will win more than they should. By the middle of the season, the bookies may have adjusted the line to reflect this, but by that time we've salted away some good money.

OTHER WINNING STRATEGIES

1. One suggestion is to know as much as you can about the baseball teams.

Another would be to concentrate on several teams once you see which way you can make money. For example, let's suppose that you're concentrating on the National League, and have really studied the National League West.

You've digested their stats, and studied their pitchers and know a great deal about their strengths and weaknesses. But for some reason, maybe the chance that this season is an anomaly, different than the last previous few season, you're not really making any money.

Meanwhile, something in the American League East has caught your eye. You see some trends that we've discussed, some situations that can make you money. So you start betting on those games, and switch your whole plan of attack, and start winning bets. Now it's these teams you're watching and studying. Fine. These things happen.

Don't hang around whipping a dead horse, when there's a live situation developing somewhere else. Don't be stubborn. Change your direction and your area of study, if that is what is making you money.

2. See as many games as you can, either in person or on TV.

This is a leisurely game, and unlike football, where it's hard to concentrate on any one aspect of the game without disregarding the others, here you can easily see what is going on. There are long intervals of no action. You can study any aspect of the game you desire at the ballpark.

3. Even if you concentrate on the American League East, for example, they'll be playing teams from all the other American League teams, so you must study those teams thoroughly.

Baseball betting requires a ton of study; if you don't have the time to do this, don't bet on the games.

4. In studying the various teams' strengths and weaknesses, in addition to the pitching, you want to know about their middle strength (catcher, shortstop, second baseman and centerfielder).

That's a key element in the game. How is their fielding? What kind of home team are they? How well do they perform on the road? Do their pitchers do well in night games? Are they better during the day?

Generally speaking, the pitchers with **heat,** the live fast ball, do better at night, because it's harder for a batter to see the ball. However, in some parks, the layout is such that the batter's vision is obscured by spectators wearing white in the centerfield seats. Study all these situations.

5. When betting, don't go over 2% of your bankroll on any game.

Move up only if you're winning money. If you're losing, stop betting, don't increase your bets. And don't bet if it's hurting you financially or emotionally.

6. Keep records.

You should have a rundown the pitchers in the league, their starts, their stats, whether they won or lost, whom they won or lost to, or if there was no decision. If no decision, whether the team won or lost. Keep whatever records you need to guide you in correct betting.

Keep records on the teams themselves. A lot of information may be gotten from *USA Today* , your local newspaper or better yet, *The Sporting News* . Study and keep studying. Baseball is a fascinating game for that reason; you can never probe deep enough to find a new angle that will make you money.

7. Shop for value.

By this we mean getting the best price you can. Suppose you want to bet on the Padres at Los Angeles. Your bookie, or if you live in Vegas, the sports book you usually bet at quotes the game as follows:

LOS ANGELES -1.50 San Diego +1.30

This means that a bet on the Padres will give you $1.30 for every dollar you bet. However, in shopping around, you get another quote:

LOS ANGELES -1.60 San Diego +1.40

Now you're getting 1.40 for each dollar, You're getting more value betting on the dog here. Conversely, if you're betting on the favorite, you'd want the original quote of 1.50 on the Dodgers. It's more value to you to lay 1.50 than to lay 1.60. You can get value a great deal of the time. Don't rush your bet, shop it around.

C. Over and Under Betting

A number will generally be put up for each game played in the majors, the "Over and Under Number." The number may be 7 or 8 or an odd number such as 71/2, where the bookies are assured that there will be no push involved.

When betting under and over, it's of vital importance to not only study the pitching, but the number of runs each team is capable of producing on average over the season.

In the American League, with the DH rule, with nine good batters in the lineup instead of eight and a weak-hitting pitcher, more runs are scored, and the number is higher.

Again, you have to do a great deal of studying to be secure with your bets. How did the team do against this particular pitcher last time out?

How well are the pitchers doing now? Are they both sharp or both in decline? Is one sharp and the other weak? How about the hitting? Is one of the teams in a slump? Are both in a slump?

The past stats will give you a good idea of just where the number should be on over and under bets, but you must refine it further by knowing just how the team is performing now.

Here's where injuries are really important to know about, because if the key slugger is out of the lineup, the run production may fall away dramatically.

In Over and Under betting, you're giving the bookie a 4.54% edge because you're laying 11-10, whether you go over or under against the number.

Like all other betting, make mind bets against the number till you can be sure that you win enough times to show a profit. With an 11-1 line you must win at least 53% of the time to show any sort of profit.

D. Money Management

It's more difficult when betting baseball to know exactly where you stand in terms of profit and losses, because a few losses when betting a favorite can dent the bankroll.

In football or basketball betting, you're working with a strict 4.54 liability. In baseball, the bookie's edge changes with the money line quote, and it alters whether you bet on the favorite or decide to wager on the underdog. But it's not only this edge that you have to worry about.

If you're betting on the favorite, you must win more times than you lose, sometimes, as in a 1.50-1 wager, 20 percentage points more, and then you only break even!

We've touched on various things you should do, such as shopping for value, never making a bet where you're giving more than 1.60-1. We can't afford to try to win 63% of the time with those bets.

Our best suggestion is not to make actual wagers till the season has been underway for at least a month, and you find that you show a profit with imaginary bets alone. Whatever your bankroll, if you find that mind bets have depleted it by 20%, don't bet real cash. Restudy your strategies for betting. you're doing something wrong.

Only when you show a profit, step in with real cash.

We suggest never betting more than 2% of your bankroll on any one game for awhile, unless you see that you're winning consistently. Then you can increase it steadily till you get to 5% of your bankroll. As you win, increase the betting range, and as you lose, decrease it. If you reach a point where you're losing money for the season, stop betting. Restudy the principles you're betting by.

When we say bet 2% of your bankroll, it becomes a tricky thing. Let's say this calls for a $200 wager. If you're betting on the underdog and getting 1.30 on that bet you'll win $360. If you bet on the favorite and lay 1.50, you'll be getting only $133 for your $200 wager, if you win.

The bookie may not take the odd $200 bet when the money line is 1.50-1. He may require $225 be placed so the payoff is exactly $150 rather than the odd amount shown for the $200 bet. So you may have to alter your bets slightly.

Keep a running count on your profits or losses. Divide your winnings or losses when betting on the favorites or the dogs. See which way brings you more money. You may find you have a knack for the dogs and you're going down the drain betting on favorites. Stick to the dogs.

The Gambling Maniac's Diary, (order form in the back) provides a handy place to keep your records.

Or vice versa. Remember, there's plenty of action available. Pick your spots and be patient, and go with the kind of bets that work for you. Suppose you find that you can pick 60% of the over and under games. Stick with these and increase your bets up to 5% or more, if you're a consistent winner.

Why fool around with picking winners of individual games when you have the gift of picking under and over games?

Always keep in mind that you're in this to make money. Baseball betting is complex and requires a lot of study. To be successful you almost have to love the game, because you'll be immersed in all its variables day after day.

If you can't devote the time to the game, don't bet it, because it'll be hard to make correct judgments without all sorts of knowledge and information. But if you can win by study, great! Baseball affords a lot of action on a daily basis, and the winnings can really add up tremendously!

E. THE MAJOR LEAGUE TEAMS AND THEIR BALLPARKS

THE AMERICAN LEAGUE

The American League is known as the "junior circuit", having been formed some years after the National League.

It has the designated hitter rule, which means that the pitcher need not bat. As a result, more runs are scored in the American League, and the ERAs of the pitchers is slightly higher than in the National League. The DH rule allows teams with aging but powerful hitters to do nothing but bat. They never have to field and can rest between innings.

AMERICAN LEAGUE - EAST

Baltimore Orioles
They play on natural grass in Memorial Stadium. For many

years they were known for their solid pitching and defense. This was important, because basically Memorial Stadium is known as a pitcher's park, where the field breaks sharply in the power alleys.

Boston Red Sox

The Red Sox play in Fenway Park, an aging structure and a delight for right-handed hitters. Any right-handed hitter with power will increase his average tremendously in this park with its inviting "green monster," a fence 37 feet high 315 feet from home plate.

The field is natural grass, and for years Boston featured mediocre fielding infielders with power, such as Junior Stephens. As a result of its left field fence, it is a lateral graveyard for left-handed pitchers. Very few managers will take a chance and pitch southpaws here.

Cleveland Indians

They play in Cleveland Stadium, with short left and right field foul lines, on natural grass. Many times in recent years, the Tribe has been hyped up as a contender, only to disappoint its fans. Their park is a decaying relic, known as The Mistake by the Lake.

Detroit Tigers

The Tigers play their games in Tiger Stadium, on natural grass. A team with southpaw sluggers generally has a field day here, but it's a hitter's park for all sluggers.

Milwaukee Brewers

The Brewers are best when they have power hitters, for the bounds of County Stadium, where they play on natural grass, is a haven for sluggers. The Brewers are known for their fine organization, which has helped the club get and keep good talent.

New York Yankees

The Yankees play on natural grass in Yankee Stadium, the "House that Babe Ruth built." Of all baseball teams, this one has the greatest tradition, with players such as Babe Ruth,, Lou Gehrig and Joe DiMaggio starring for legendary teams. There's plenty of money behind the ownership, but George Steinbrenner's meddling ways have certainly hurt the team, with constant feuds and battles going on between management and the players and managers.

The Stadium favors left-field hitters, while left field slopes away sharply, hurting hitters with right-handed power.

Toronto Blue Jays

The Blue Jays have a new stadium, an enclosed one called The Sky Dome. Since they were admitted into the major leagues, the Blue Jays have been a consistently successful organization, fielding solid teams year after year.

They don't have the trouble that Montreal has in getting good players to stay with the organization, despite the weakness of the Canadian dollar. Their fine management keeps the team viable season after season.

AMERICAN LEAGUE - WEST

California Angels

The foul lines in Anaheim Stadium extend to 333 feet in both directions, making this a tough hitting park. The Angels try to take advantage of this situation with good solid. It is truly a hurler's stadium.

Despite the money that Gene Autry, the owner, pours in to get top talent, the Angels have been a constant disappointment. But money alone isn't sufficient to get a World Series ring; what the Angels need is some good baseball minds to put together a winner.

Chicago White Sox

With the foul lines extending 352 feet down both sides, pull hitters get quickly discouraged. When you hit a home run in Comiskey Park, you have to really bat the ball.

However, power hitters get a wide target with the generous proportions of the field, for center field extends out to 445 feet.

The owners of recent vintage, Reinsdorf and Einhorn, aren't baseball men, and have done little to strengthen the club since they assumed control. Some clear baseball minds would help the Chisox a great deal.

Kansas City Royals

The Royals play on Tartan Turf in Royals Stadium and as a result of the artificial surface, ground balls are a hazard to fielders' healthy fielding averages. The balls skip and bounce their way through the infield and keep going to the wall in many cases.

The owner, Ewing Kaufman, is a responsible owner, and he has paid good money to his players and brought in top talent, so that the Royals are consistent contenders in the AL West. He's particularly good at buying and trading for top pitching.

Minnesota Twins

The Twins play at the Metrodome, also known as the "Homerdome." It's a domed stadium with artificial surfaces, and a hitter's paradise. The Twins build their teams to accommodate the park, and usually have a terrific winning percentage at home.

Oakland A's

They play in Oakland Coliseum on natural grass, in a field fair to both hitters and pitchers.

The A's have concentrated on the same balance in their ballclubs. The Levi Strauss Company, which owns the A's, is not afraid to put tons of money behind the club, and their future looks assured for years to come.

Seattle Mariners

The Mariners play in the Kingdome, on an artificial surface, and as usual with domed stadiums, it is a good solid hitters' park.

Now all the Mariners need are good hitters to take advantage of the park. They've been pretty much a non-entity since they entered the league as an expansion club, and most experts seem to feel they've long way to go to be a contender in the

Texas Rangers

With previous management practically giving away all the talent on this club, the Rangers have had their problems in recent years. They've got a ton of rebuilding to do to get this club moving again.

The Rangers play in Arlington Stadium, a neutral park as far as hurlers or sluggers go, on natural grass.

NATIONAL LEAGUE

The "Senior Circuit" still plays baseball the old fashioned way. There is no DH rule, and thus whether or not to remove a pitcher for a hitter in crucial situations remains a key strategy.

In the National League, it's more difficult for a pitcher to complete a game, because he's in danger of being yanked in a close game, particularly in the late innings.

NATIONAL LEAGUE EAST

Chicago Cubs

Winds affect Wrigley Field, that ancient stadium the Cubbies play in. In the early part of the season, the wind blows into home plate, and the advantage is to the pitchers. Later on in the season, it blows out to the stands. Advantage batters. After resisting lights for many years, the Cubs finally play night ball at their park.

In the early years of the National League, the Cubs owned a lot of pennants, but they've been real disappointments to their loyal fans since then.

Montreal Expos

The Expos have had problems holding onto players because of the foreignness of their area, which is mostly French speaking, and the weakness of the Canadian dollar. As soon as a player is eligible for free agency, he's gone. Yet, with the talent remaining, they come up as contenders.

They play their games in Olympic Stadium, on the artificial surface, a park known as a hitter's park.

New York Mets

The Mets are either pulling miracles out of the air, as in their 6th

145

game World Series victory over the Red Sox in 1986 when the champagne was being poured in the Red Sox clubhouse, or they're disappointing their fans by not living up to their strength as a team.

It's a real roller coaster ride being a Mets fan. They've been known for great pitching, always coming up with a new young star hurler, such as Dwight Gooden. Yet they've traded away future Hall of Famers like Nolan Ryan.

The great pitching helps them in a pitcher's park like Shea Stadium, where they play on natural grass. Bettors have found some soft spots betting against the Mets, who are hyped up by the New York media, only to end up as also-rans.

Philadelphia Phillies

The Phillies play at Veteran Stadium, on an artificial surface. It's a big field, but is considered neutral, favoring neither pitchers or hitters.

The team surprises every now and then. It's an interesting team to watch at the beginning of the season, when they can fashion a winning record that usually doesn't hold up.

Pittsburgh Pirates

The Pirates play on an artificial surface in Three Rivers Stadium. It's a field that favors left-handed sluggers, and when the Pirates have this kind of power they're formidable at home.

The team has been rebuilding in the last few years and should soon come together and make a run at the pennant any season now.

St. Louis Cardinals

This is a team that has concentrated on a great deal of speed and a strong defense, which has stood it in good stead over the years. With a strong organization behind them in the form of the Busch family, the Cardinals are well supported. They have a proud tradition as well, and must be considered a factor in future season.

The play at Busch Memorial Stadium, on an artificial surface, which is ideal for their speed and for such superstar defense men as Ozzie Smith.

National League West

Atlanta Braves

Like all the Atlanta franchises run by Ted Turner, the Braves suffer from having an owner who has given this club no real direction. It's a good team to bet against, for they find comfort deep in their division, usually in the cellar.

The Braves play in Fulton County Stadium on natural grass. With only 6 foot walls in left and right fields, and winds blowing out to the stands most of the time, it is known as a hitter's ballpark.

Cincinnati Reds

With the scandal about Pete Rose's gambling making the headlines most of the 1989 season, with the clubhouse flooded with media people, the Reds were a bit distracted, to say the least. Now that Pete Rose is gone as manager, the club has been able to play to its potential.

Its games are played in Riverfront Stadium, on an artificial surface. Though the field is considered neutral, the Reds have built an organization featuring sluggers and hard hitters, and who can ever forget the glory days of the "Big Red Machine," when their lineup put fear into all the other NL pitching staffs.

Houston Astros

The Astrodome has a reputation of preventing batters from hitting for distance. As a result, its not only the home of the Astros, but of many low scoring games. To take advantage of this situation, the Astros have always tried to have good pitching and a solid defense.

Although the organization has fashioned a good farm system, it hasn't sent up the men to make the Astros a contender. Their needs over the years always focused on power, getting power hitters or hitters, period. It's still their big need.

Los Angeles Dodgers

The Dodgers play on natural grass before loyal fans who come by the millions every season and bring their radios along, tuning

147

into Vince Scully, the broadcaster, as if they can't figure out the game just by watching it.

The Dodgers have always concentrated on good pitching, but trades and injuries have decimated their staff. They have a money laden organization behind them, and the club likes to win in the major TV market it operates in.

A lot of action comes to the Dodgers in Las Vegas which thinks of the Dodgers and their home club.

San Diego Padres

Now that Ray Kroc, the former owner, is dead, and his widow has taken over the club, it pretty much in the hands of its general manager and others. Jack McKeon loved to trade players, and he was terrific at trading away solid pitching, with disastrous results.

The team plays on natural grass in a big park, Jack Murphy Stadium, which is considered neutral for pitching and hitting.

San Francisco Giants

The owners keep threatening to move the club out of San Francisco unless a new park is built for them. Candlestick Park, where they play, is the kind of stadium where a pitcher can be blown off the mound by the prevailing winds. However, the city of San Francisco keeps defeating bond issues which would allow such a new arena to be built.

So, hitters and fielders hope for the best here. The team has a good general manager and field manager, and a solid organization behind it.

6. COLLEGE FOOTBALL BETTING

A. THE POINTSPREAD AND LINE

College football employs the same pointspread and line as does the NFL. One team is favored over another by so many points, known as the spread, and you've got to cover the spread to win your bet. If Notre Dame is playing the University of Miami, and the line looks like this:

MIAMI -Notre Dame +3

It means that Miami, in capital letters, is at home, and is favored over Notre Dame by 3 points. To win the bet, if you bet on the favorite Hurricanes, they must win by more than 3 points. If you bet on Notre Dame, they have to lose by less than 3 points (or win the game straight-up). If the score is Miami 13- Notre Dame 10, then its a push, and nobody wins or loses.

Like the pro game, the bettor gives the bookie 11-10 on all bets, giving the bookmaker an edge or vig of 4.54%, and requiring the bettor to win at least 52.38% of his wagers just to break even.

In the NFL game, a -10 (or +10) is considered a big spread. It is rare that one team is favored over the other by more than that number of points. That's not the case in the college ranks. At times, teams like Oklahoma have been as many as 40 points favorite over some hapless opponent like Kansas State (and sometimes favored by more).

149

In the pros, the line may change, but it changes within a point or two generally. In the college game, there can be wild swings of more than 7 points in the course of a week.

Another major difference is in the number of games that are played week by week in the college game. There may be as many as 90 ʼeams on which a line is developed, though generally about 25-30 games is the rule around the country.

Compare this to the 14 games played in the NFL. This means that there's more room for error in the oddsmaker's appraisal of a particular game between college teams than there is in the NFL.

When there are errors, or "creases, " it's important that the bettor take advantage of them. But he can only do this if he's studied the situations involved and can make a correct judgment of the bookie's errors.

B. CONCENTRATING ON A FEW CONFERENCES

The surest way to beat the bookie is to know more than he does about a particular game or games. To do this, we suggest that the bettor study a few conferences, and know them cold. In order to do this he should:

1. Go back several years and study all the conference teams and their games, both in the conference and out of it.

The bettor should know how certain teams match up against other teams year after year.

Is Purdue up for the Indiana game in the Big Ten? In that same conference, how does Iowa handle Michigan State? And so forth. In that same conference for many years, Ohio State was a good bet against in the early part of the season. Under Woody Hayes, they'd often lost to non-conference rivals, then go all out against Big Ten schools.

2. Concentrate on one or two conferences. Go back through the years, study the rivalries, see how schools did at various parts of the season, at home and away, and you're going to get some important insights that the bookie might not have. You might sense something that the oddsmaker has overlooked.

3. You should, in addition to the past records, keep up with the conference during the current season.

If you can, study the hometown newspapers and the college newspapers. They'll often give you certain insights, that may be super-valuable. There may be dissension, there may be a couple of injuries that are written about. All kinds of information can be gathered that way.

Or conversely, the school may really be up for the forthcoming game, either to revenge a previous humiliation or for another reason. Read and study all you can about the conference and its teams. After all, if you pick the Ivy League, for example, and you get an insight into the Brown-Penn game, you may know more than the oddsmaker does.

C. MAKING YOUR OWN LINE

It's important to have your own line within the conference, and for those non-conference rivals that the conference team will play against and you might bet on or against. For example, Notre Dame will always play a few Big Ten rivals, such as Purdue and Michigan. You must get a line on Notre Dame for these games.

Use a rating system from 0 to whatever number the weakest team is assigned. A 0 indicates the strongest school - anything higher than that is for the weaker team. For example, in the Big Eight, you might show:

Oklahoma	0
Nebraska	1
Colorado	6

...and so forth, all the way down to Kansas State, which might be given a 40. This means that when Oklahoma plays Kansas State, theoretically Oklahoma is a 40 point favorite (43 at home; 37 away at Kansas State).

The line shouldn't be made just for fun; this is a line you're going to bet on. It should carefully be prepared from previous seasons records and from the talent the teams have this season.

It must be accurate. You may have to wait a few weeks into the season before the line jells, before you get it right. Don't bet till you see that your line is more accurate than the bookie's, and that you can make money betting on it.

The purpose of the line is to give you a basis for betting. If Nebraska is playing at Lincoln against Colorado, and you've made a line that shows Nebraska 5 points better than the Buffaloes, and you add another 3 points for the home field advantage for the Cornhuskers, then your line will read:

NEBRASKA - Colorado +8

If the official line is within one point of that line, then you can't bet the game.

Only when the official line deviates from your line by 3 or more points, should you now look seriously at the game. Suppose the official line reads:

NEBRASKA   - Colorado +3

Then, you should bet on Nebraska. You're only giving away 3 points in a game you feel should have forced you to lay 8 points. And the more the line moves away from your line, the more you should bet.

Of course, this should only be the case where you've accurately forecast games before using your line and you've won at least 53% of the time, enough to make money.

Until your line is accurate, that is, can make you money betting it, don't wager real money.

TRENDS

You must be aware of trends in college football. Certain schools just can't beat other schools or cover the spread, and this may happen 70% or more of the time. You've got to go with the trend, and not fight it.

Other trends are apparent. Schools that are going for number 1 in the polls are generally piling up the points late in the season, to impress the AP and College Coaches Polls.

Teams like Alabama, Michigan and Oklahoma, smelling that number 1 spot, start winning big and covering the spreads easily.

Other teams do the same thing. If Notre Dame is ranked number 2 and is playing Navy, you can be sure that Notre Dame is going to really whip Navy. And if the number 1 team that week is Nebraska and it's playing Kansas, too bad for the Jayhawks. Get on the bandwagon in these situations.

If you feel the trend should stop, wait and don't bet the game. Often, the trend goes on for some unknown reason.

Motivation

College teams, like the pros, get motivated. A coach may have a long memory and remember just how, two years ago, his team, weaker than it is today, was humiliated by a team its playing this Saturday. You can be sure his team will be up for that game.

Or another team, which was headed for a top ranking, was upset by a weaker school the year before. Now they're meeting again, and you can be sure that the team upset last year will go all out to avenge that defeat.

You have to be aware of these situations, and you can only do that by studying the past records and also getting a feel for the upcoming game by reading up-to-date information about the two teams.

As shown in the previous section, motivation runs rampant when a team is trying to be number 1 in the polls. It has every reason to do its best, especially against a much weaker team. Go with motivation; it's the best thing you can bet on.

COACHES

The college coach has a task that the NFL coach doesn't have. He must recruit players for his team. He can't draft them and pay them a salary; he must show them the good reason for playing at his school.

One of the best reason is the tradition of winning, of getting national exposure because of a number of TV games. The blue chip high school prospect is already thinking of the NFL - he sees that playing for a top rated team will get him the kind of exposure that spells All-American and then a big contract when he's picked in an early round of the NFL draft.

It's money, baby, we're talking about, and money makes the sports world turn.

Some coaches, even with a proud tradition behind them at the school, are hapless. A good example was Gerry Faust at Notre Dame. While he coached, the team fell apart. When Lou Holtz stepped in, they were on their way to a national championship.

Some coaches, like Bo Schlembecher, were awfully respected guys, but they couldn't win big games. In other schools, like the Miami Hurricanes, it doesn't seem to matter who coaches; the team wins anyway.

Every year, there are periodicals devoted to the recruiting process and records are kept of recruited players. A survey will show which team recruited best. Study this and get an early insight into the future strength of the school's team.

D. Money Management

We always suggest, first, that you bet only with money you can afford to lose, and that can't hurt you if you lose it. Here are other things to keep in mind.

1. Don't bet for the first few weeks of the season until your imaginary or mind bets win at least 53% of the time.

2. Never bet more than 2% of your bankroll on any one game until you've formed a winning pattern.

Then increase the bets up to 5% for the first season. After that, you can bet according to the formula we showed in the NFL section. To refresh your recollection, you can bet up to 5% of your bankroll with a 55% winning percentage - and that would be the maximum.

3. If you encounter a losing streak, lower your bets.

Don't fight the streak. If you find you can't win 53% of the time, stop betting and rethink your lines.

4. Bet for value.

If your line is accurate, the more the official line moves away from it, the more you bet. If the line moves towards your line, stop betting.

Thus, if you picked Missouri over Iowa State by 9 and the line is 5, you have a good bet on Missouri. If the official line moves to 3, you have another bet on Missouri. But if the line moves to Missouri by 8 or 9, you can't bet the game. There's no edge for you.

5. Like the pros, bet on the favorite early in the week, and the underdog later in the week.

As a general rule, you'll get better value for your bet this way.

6. Shop around for value.

In the college game, a team may go for one or two points after the touchdown. Often this is the whole difference between winning or losing a bet.

If you want to bet on the dog, and are offered 9 points by one bookie, shop around. Or if you're in Vegas, go to other sports books. You may get 10 or 101/2 or 11 points. Those extra points sometimes makes the difference between a winning or losing season.

7. Finally, be patient.

Don't look just for action, look to win money. Pick your conferences or teams, and study them, and only if the spot is good, make the bet. Don't just bet to get excitement or because the game is on TV.

If you follow all these principles of money management, you'll end up a winner!

E. THE STRUCTURE OF COLLEGE FOOTBALL

COLLEGE FOOTBALL'S STRUCTURE

Most teams that compete in intercollegiate football belong to conferences, with some independent of any affiliation. For the most part conferences are organized with a geographic thread running through the conference.

For example, the **Big Ten** is composed of most of the land grant colleges in the Midwest, the upper Midwest. The schools in this conference are fairly strong academically, and a few, such as Illinois, Michigan and Northwestern, rank with the very best in the country.

Likewise, the **Ivy League**, with its emphasis on academics, is made up of schools within a fairly tight geographical location, running from the New England states to Pennsylvania.

The **Pacific Coast Conference** runs up and down the Pacific and into the bordering state of Arizona. And so forth.

Still, there are other schools, such as Notre Dame, which have decided to remain independent of any conference. In fact, Notre Dame, with its great tradition in college football, has worked a TV deal that is the envy of all other schools in the NCAA.

In the next sections, we'll rundown practically all the schools you'll be able to bet on, conference by conference, and the independents as well. Within a conference, the talent dispersal may be unbalanced. For example, Michigan, in the Big Ten, is a powerhouse year after year, while Northwestern, in the same conference, is a doormat.

This factor has to do with any number of things. Michigan has a winning tradition in football, something Northwestern is not concerned about. Losing programs begat other losing programs.

In the **Pac 10** (Pacific Coast Conference) a team like USC, with its great rivalries against Notre Dame and UCLA, will get exposure on National TV, while Oregon State gets practically no TV exposure. Great athletes will want to go to a school like USC where they'll be seen all over the land, rather than to Oregon State where they'll molder in obscurity.

Sometimes a program will be revitalized at a school because of a new coach and his recruiting policies. However, this may create permanent and long-reaching difficulties as many schools have found out when put on NCAA probation for recruitment violations on the part of coaches.

When listing the various colleges, we'll also list their location, to make it easier for those who might want to study the local newspapers or college papers.

ATLANTIC COAST CONFERENCE

In this conference, basketball is king, with football playing a secondary role. The football played in the ACC is generally mediocre, with teams like Wake Forest, Virginia and Georgia Tech seen as patsy's against strong schools outside the conference.

Now and then one of the colleges in the ACC catches fire, as did Clemson in 1981, and goes on to national prominence. In that year, Clemson won the national championship.

Despite their mediocre records, the schools have fanatical fans, and they usually rise at home games beyond their theoretical expectations.

School	Location
Clemson	Clemson, South Carolina
Duke	Durham, North Carolina
Georgia Tech	Atlanta, Georgia
Maryland	College Park, Maryland
North Carolina	Chapel Hill, North Carolina
North Carolina State	Raleigh, North Carolina
Virginia	Charlottesville, Virginia
Wake Forest	Winston Salem, North Carolina

BIG EIGHT

Year after year, Nebraska and Oklahoma emerge as powerhouses, striking fear into other football teams throughout the nation, and especially to the weak schools within the conference. As strong as the Cornhuskers and Sooners are, so, on the other hand, are Kansas State, Kansas and Iowa State generally weak.

The conference schools are located in the Midwest and parts of the Southwest.

The better schools, football speaking, are known to pamper their athletes inordinately, to the point that the NCAA has put its foot down for infractions both in recruiting and for other violations. Oklahoma is a prime example of a school cited for violations.

Schools	Location
Colorado	Boulder, Colorado
Iowa State	Ames, Iowa
Kansas	Lawrence, Kansas
Kansas State	Manhattan, Kansas
Missouri	Columbia, Missouri
Nebraska	Lincoln, Nebraska
Oklahoma	Norman, Oklahoma
Oklahoma State	Stillwater, Oklahoma

BIG TEN

With most of the schools located in the proximity of the Great Lakes, this conference excels at both athletics and academics.

Two schools basically dominate the football programs in the Big Ten - Michigan and Ohio State. The Wolverines seem to make a run for the national championship year after year, without success. Ohio State's Buckeyes have been perennial powers, but have fallen down a bit since Woody Hayes was fired as coach some years back.

Now and then another school rises up to national prominence. The Conference champion meets the champion of the Pac 10 in the Rose Bowl each year. In recent years, the Pac 10 has dominated this rivalry, and the grinding pattern of football the Big 10 is known for may be way out-of-date. It may be characterized as "3 yards and a cloud of dust."

School	Location
Illinois	Champaign-Urbana, Illinois
Indiana	Bloomington, Indiana
Iowa	Iowa City, Iowa
Michigan	Ann Arbor, Michigan
Michigan State	East Lansing, Michigan
Minnesota	Minneapolis, Minnesota
Northwestern	Evanston, Illinois
Ohio State	Columbus, Ohio
Purdue	Lafayette, Indiana
Wisconsin	Madison, Wisconsin

IVY LEAGUE

At one time this was the conference that produced national championships, but that was a long time ago, back in the 1920s and 1930s. By that time the tradition of great football has been going on in the Ivy League all the way back to he beginning of the 20th Century.

In those days, of course, the teams were made up of true student-athletes, which they still are in the Ivy League. However, in the rest of the country, illiteracy is generally not a detriment to becoming a student at a football factory, otherwise knows as a university. And so the Ivy League, which is preeminent in academics in America, has declined as a football league.

The rivalries are intense, particularly the biggest game of all, Harvard-Yale.

For some odd reason, Ivy League football is given a line by the bookmakers, even though the games aren't of high caliber. This is one conference I recommend studying, for if you know the makeup of the teams and their relative strengths, you should be able to fashion a winning line here.

School	Location
Brown	Providence, Rhode Island
Columbia	New York, New York
Cornell	Ithaca, New York
Dartmouth	Hanover, New Hampshire
Harvard	Cambridge, Massachusetts
Pennsylvania	Philadelphia, Pennsylvania
Princeton	Princeton, New Jersey
Yale	New Haven, Connecticut

PACIFIC 10

The Pac 10 has become a strong football conference with its mainstays, USC and UCLA able to hold their own against the best in the country. In addition to these powerful schools, others in the Pac 10 rise up from time to time to national prominence, teams such as the Washington Huskies and the Arizona State Sun Devils.

The conference champion plays the Big 10 champion in the Rose Bowl each New Year's Day. The Rose Bowl is the oldest of the bowl games, but its luster has faded with this Pac 10-Big 10 rivalry, for it rarely produces a national champion.

More often, the winner of the Orange, Sugar or Cotton Bowl, and in recent years, the Fiesta Bowl, has produced a national champion.

School	Location
Arizona	Tucson, Arizona
Arizona State	Tempe, Arizona
California	Berkeley, California
Oregon	Eugene, Oregon
Oregon State	Corvallis, Oregon
Stanford	Palo Alto, California
UCLA	Westwood, California
USC	Los Angeles, California
Washington	Seattle, Washington
Washington State	Pullman, Washington

SOUTHEASTERN CONFERENCE

The conference stretches from the border states of Tennessee and Kentucky through the deep South. For many years, their dominant football power was Alabama, which, under Bear Bryant, put out a number of national champions. Other teams, such as Georgia, Florida and LSU have also received national attention.

The conference fans take their football very seriously, and are rather rabid about their loyalty to their teams. Home field advantages mean quite a bit here.

There have been a number of recruiting and other violations in this conference, particularly against Florida. A private school like Vanderbilt, with its fine academic standing, has often been a doormat in these conference.

School	Location
Alabama	University, Alabama
Auburn	Auburn,Alabama
Florida	Gainesville, Florida
Georgia	Athens, Georgia
Kentucky	Lexington, Kentucky
LSU	Baton Rouge, Louisiana
Mississippi	Oxford, Mississippi
Mississippi State	State College, Mississippi
Tennessee	Knoxville, Tennessee
Vanderbilt	Nashville, Tennessee

SOUTHWESTERN CONFERENCE

This could just as well be called the Texas Conference, for eight of its nine members are Texas schools. The lone exception is Arkansas.

Its a strong football conference, but one that has a long history of NCAA violations, and some teams, such as SMU have been given the "death penalty," eliminating football as a viable sport for a number of years.

Still, the intense recruiting goes on, probably because so many of the schools are vying for the same Texas football talent.

A big rivalry outside the conference is Texas-Oklahoma, but in recent years the Texas football program has weakened, and they're not one of the perennial powers anymore. The Arkansas Razorbacks however, still field strong teams year after year.

School	Location
Arkansas	Fayettesville, Arkansas
Baylor	Waco, Texas
Houston	Houston, Texas
Rice	Houston, Texas
SMU	Dallas, Texas
Texas	Austin, Texas
Texas A&M	College Station, Texas
Texas Christian	Fort Worth, Texas
Texas Tech	Lubbock, Texas

INDEPENDENT SCHOOLS

Several of the independents are real football powers, and make a bid for the national championship year after year. Schools like Notre Dame, Miami, Florida State, Penn State, and occasionally one of the others will be in the headlines week after week during football season.

Many of the independents prefer to have a national schedule and not be bound to play at least six of their games against conference rivals, as is the situation with conference teams.

The three service academies are among the independents for they are obligated to play national schedules for the most part, though they have regional rivalries as well.

It has been many years since any of those three teams made a run for the national title. They can't recruit on the same level as other football teams, and no longer is free tuition and then a stint in the Armed Forces an inducement to youngsters coming out of high school with great athletic ability.

These days, the best athletes are pointing to the big bucks in the

NFL. That is the supreme goal of practically all of them, with the colleges forming a free minor league for the pros. Of course, the colleges benefit also. There is big money wherever TV coverage is involved.

The following independents usually are listed in the official line put out by Vegas week after week.

School	Location
Air Force	Colorado Springs, Colorado
Army	West Point, New York
Boston College	Boston, Massachusetts
Florida State	Tallahassee, Florida
Memphis State	Memphis, Tennessee
Miami	Miami, Florida
Navy	Annapolis, Maryland
Notre Dame	South Bend, Indiana
Penn State	University Park, Pennsylvania
Pittsburgh	Pittsburgh, Pennsylvania
South Carolina	Columbia, South Carolina
Syracuse	Syracuse, New York
Tulane	New Orleans, Louisiana
Virginia Tech	Blacksburg, Virginia
West Virginia	Morgantown, West Virginia

BOWL GAMES AND RIVALRIES

After the regular season, there's a plethora of bowl games available to bet on. Many of these come about in December, with the very big bowls, such as the Rose and Orange, occurring on New Year's Day.

Usually there will be a few soft spots that bettors can take advantage of. For many years, Michigan, under coach Bo Schlembecher, couldn't win the last game of the season, the bowl game, and with good reason. The coach was a respected man, but his abilities left much to be desired. He could recruit fabulous players but in his system of old-fashioned offense, they sputtered like a dying engine.

The Pac 10 teams they played for the most part were ready for them, and featured innovative systems. It became an embarrassment year after year for the followers of the Wolverines. Now Bo has resigned but his successor vows to continue in his footsteps.

We expect Michigan's trend of failing at the end to continue. Don't go against trends unless they finally reverse and are no longer applicable. Trends can make money for you, and no one is clairvoyant enough to know when they'll stop.

Other soft spots occur when a team is touted by the media to be a national power, such as West Virginia in 1988 and Colorado in 1989. The papers had a field day with these squads, but in the end, they couldn't really cut the cake when playing against the best in a bowl game.

Look for the hype and go against it. Colorado as a national champion would have made a lovely story because of the untimely death of their quarterback at the beginning of the 1989 season. But it wasn't to be. And Major Harris, touted as a tremendous quarterback for the Mountaineers of West Virginia, was shown to be less than tremendous, and in fact, in the NFL draft, he went last among all the quarterbacks chosen.

The NFL doesn't listen to hype; they have to see what a player can really do.

So look for these mismatches. Just as in the NFL, the betting public has a certain distorted perception of what the teams can do, often fed by loyalty or media. Go against the betting public whenever you can, because they're practically always wrong.

As to rivalries - college football abounds with them. Army-Navy, Harvard-Yale, Michigan-Ohio State, Notre Dame-Southern Cal, USC-UCLA, Alabama-Auburn and on and on.

My feeling is that anything can happen during these games, and usually anything does happen. Unless one squad is clearly better than the other, which has had a bad season, it usually pay to go with the underdog.

If both teams can make a game of it, there are enough upsets to warrant betting on the dog. I've found that not only have I won a lot of these bets, but in many cases, the underdog upset the favorite straight-up. Study rivalries with extra care. Don't bet on the dogs blindly, but look for your spots.

With all the action available in the college game, with all those schools and games to choose from, a smart bettor armed with information can have a field day!

7. PRO BASKETBALL

A. INTRODUCTION

Basketball gives us a mixture of football and baseball when it comes to wagering. Football, because it uses a similar line, based on a pointspread, with one team favored over another by so many points. Baseball, because there is action every day during the season.

In fact, with 27 pro teams (with more coming on board in the coming years) and well over 150 college teams participating in the sport, the bettor has the widest selection of bets available in any American sport.

Oddsmakers, in order to produce a viable line, must evaluate the teams and come up with a number that will attract action on both sides - to do this, they must have an idea of the point differential between the two squads in terms of talent.

For example, if they've given the Pistons a 0 and the Hawks a 14, then Detroit, on talent, should be a 14 point favorite.

Then they must look at the home court advantage. If Atlanta is playing at home and they rate the home court advantage as 3, then Detroit should be an 11 point favorite.

Other factors may play a role. Injuries would have to be taken into consideration. Is Detroit at the beginning or end of a road trip? Everything is weighed. Is there a lot of money following the Pistons?

The final number will reflect all these factors. A final number of 9 may attract equal money. That's the bookie's goal.

Now, you must think like the bookie. If you feel that Detroit is weary, you may go with Atlanta. If Detroit is fighting for the best record in its conference, it might be worth more than 9 points.

There's no magic formula here. The thing to do is evaluate each game individually - to study each individual game.

Powerful teams cannot sustain a top-fight type of game throughout 82 games. They have to coast at times. There may be a pattern to this. They may coast at the end of a road trip, or in the middle. They may play hard for the first couple of road games, fighting to win, so they can coast later.

You must study each teams method of play. Find patterns in their play and see if they repeat.If you can be in synch with the rhythm of an NBA team, you're way ahead of the game.

The bookie has to put up a number for each game, but you don't have to bet each game. You can pick your spots - betting only on those situations where your knowledge and insight is superior to the bookie's.

That's the way to win NBA basketball bets.

If a lot of money going on the Pistons, the oddsmakers is going to penalize its backers. Perhaps that fact alone will give you sufficient value to bet on the Hawks. Perhaps not. But its something you should be aware of.

B. The Pointspread and Line

Whether you decide to bet on the pros of the college teams, or a combination of both, the same kind of line is used. It's a pointspread, and you have to give the bookie 11-10 on each bet, whether you're betting on one team to win, or making an Over and Under wager.

As we know from football, an 11-10 wager means that the bookmaker has an edge of 4.54%, his "vig" on all wagers.

Therefore, the player must win at least 53% of the time to make some money. The break even point is 52.38%. Below this percentage, a gambler will lose money. Above that percentage he'll make money. The bigger the percentage, the more money he'll make.

Let's once more show how a pointspread works. Let's assume that the Charlotte Hornets are playing the Mavericks at Dallas, and Dallas has been installed as an 8 point favorite. The official line would read:

DALLAS   Charlotte +8

The fact that Dallas is in capital letters shows that it is the home team. The +8 show what the underdog (always shown last) is given in the way of points. If Dallas wins by more than 8 points, those who bet on the Mavericks win their bet. If it wins by less than the +8, then the Hornet bettors will be cashing winning tickets. If the game ends with a score such as 123-115, right on the 8 number, then it's a "push, " with neither side winning or losing.

Over and Under bets can also be made on the games. A number is given out by the bookmaker, and you can either bet over or under that number.

For example, suppose that the Sacramento Kings are playing the Minnesota Timberwolves at Sacramento. The bookie puts up an over and under number of 220.

If you bet over, the combined total of points scored by both clubs must exceed 220 for you to win your bet. If it is less than 220, you lose your wager. If it is exactly at 220, it's a "push", and you get your money back. If you had bet under, then you'd want the teams' combined score to be below 220 so that you can win your bet.

You don't care who wins the game, only the final score.

You can also make teaser bets in basketball. The usual teaser bonus points are 4, which gives the player the right to either add these 4 points to an underdog, or subtract them from a favorite. To do this, the gambler must tease two games, and win both to cash in a winning ticket.

Let's show an example of this. There are two games you want to bet on, the first with the favorite and the second with the underdog. The line reads as follows:

PHILADELPHIA   Boston +3
CLEVELAND   Golden State +5

You make a tease bet, selecting Philadelphia and Golden State.

With the first game you now have a +1 with Boston now the favorite. By making the teaser bet, you've taken away 4 points from the 76ers, who were 3 point favorites, leaving them as underdogs by 1 point.

In the second game, you now have Golden State by +9, since you've added the four points to the +5 they already had.

Is it now a good bet? Well, the NBA brand of basketball is fast, with high scoring games. There's the 3 point play which can make up any deficit in a matter of seconds, By betting that two teams will win their games, the odds against you are 3-1, and you're laying even-money (standard on two game teasers).

It's a hard choice you have to make with teaser bets. In the NBA, where it's difficult to get a solid fix on any team on any night, picking one is hard enough; picking two to win is quite difficult. Our feeling is to avoid teasers and to concentrate on picking individual teams to win ball games. Four points is nothing at all in the NBA.

Also avoid teasers of more than two games and any parlays that the bookies will entice you with. They're all bad bets - save your money for those spots you've handicapped properly, that will bring you the long green.

Since there's so much action in basketball during its long season, the line must come out every day from Las Vegas. And it does. By 9AM, it's sent out throughout the country, and the bookies can now accept bets.

In the pros, with only 27 teams, the line will be fairly tight. Not all teams play every day. But with about 160 college teams out there all over the place, many of them obscure and small schools, the line may very well be quite loose, with a lot of creases in it. It's something to look at in depth.

C. THE NBA TEAMS

The NBA, the pros, are presently divided into two conferences, with two divisions within each conference. It's a fluid league, constantly expanding and moving about from city to city. Recently, four expansion clubs were added in Miami, Orlando, Minnesota and Charlotte.

Here's the makeup of the NBA:

EASTERN CONFERENCE

ATLANTIC DIVISION
Boston Celtics
Miami Heat
New Jersey Nets
New York Knicks
Philadelphia 76ers
Washington Bullets

CENTRAL DIVISION
Atlanta Hawks
Chicago Bulls
Cleveland Cavaliers
Detroit Pistons
Indiana Pacers
Milwaukee Bucks
Orlando Magic

WESTERN CONFERENCE

MIDWEST DIVISION
Charlotte Hornets
Dallas Mavericks
Houston Rockets
Minnesota Timberwolves
San Antonio Spurs
Utah Jazz

PACIFIC DIVISION
Golden State Warriors
Los Angeles Clippers
Los Angeles Lakers
Phoenix Suns
Portland Trail Blazers
Sacramento Kings
Seattle Supersonics

The four expansion clubs have had their difficulties , and their fans will have to be patient, for it usually takes several years before they can even approach .500 ball.

During the 1980s, two teams dominated the NBA; the Celtics and the Lakers. Both had outstanding players, with Boston featuring Larry Bird, and the Lakers Magic Johnson.

The NBA has a very long season, starting with pre-season play in the early fall, then extending through an 82 game season, ending with the playoffs which extend all the way into June.

Really, there are two seasons in the NBA - the regular one and then the playoffs. The ultimate champion of the NBA is the winner of the playoffs. It could be a team that finished third in its division, but if it comes out on top in the playoffs, it is the reigning champion.

To study the NBA Schedule in advance, a free copy may be obtained by writing to the NBA, 645 Fifth Avenue, New York, N.Y 10022.

D. Handicapping the NBA Teams

In order to bet on the NBA teams intelligently, it would be important to rank the teams according to their strength and the value of their home court. Even within these categories, there are teams that play better against certain clubs, and teams, such as the Boston Celtics, who are extremely strong at home, particularly against the Knicks. So each game can't be blindly handicapped; these factors must be weighed in.

There are a number of publications you can turn to in order to find out as much as you can about the stats, and to get a picture of the relative strengths of the teams for any upcoming season. I would suggest *The Gold Sheet*, out of Los Angeles, and *H.H. College and Pro Basketball Times*, which is published in Lawton, Oklahoma.

There are other books on the subject as well as magazines published prior to the pro basketball season. To get a list of all these periodicals, it would pay to contact the *Gambler's Book Club*, Las Vegas, NV. Their address is 630 So. 11th St., Box 4115, Las Vegas, NV 89127.

In order to make a comparative rating of the clubs on the NBA, you must have access to a great many stats and records. You should keep a record of the wins and losses home and away, the records against individual clubs home and away, the pointspreads and how the teams fared against them.

In addition, you should keep up-to-the-minute records as the season progresses, including the won-lost records of the last ten games, any streaks that have developed against the spread, either winning or losing.

If you're going to bet on the teams over and under, then you should know what to expect in any arena between any two teams. History may or may not repeat itself, but you'll have a good idea of what previous scores added up to, and this will permit you to bet intelligently.

When ranking the clubs, you can use any system that helps you.

Perhaps give the best club a "0" ranking, and go down from there, in terms of points, not just a ranking. In other words, the 27th club shouldn't just be ranked "27" but should be ranked within the number of points it is expected to lose to the best team.

For example, the 27th ranked club may only be 20 points weaker than the best club. If the best club is ranked "0", then the 27th club will be given a "20" in that case (20-0=20 point difference).

The *Gold Sheet* also gives the best club a "0" rating, and you can compare your ratings with theirs. You should use a rating system that works for you, and allows you to see at a glance just what the difference between the two clubs really is.

With the advent of computers, you can get this information put on a disk, or subscribe to information services that already have computerized information. Just look into any basketball periodical for this. There are usually plenty of advertisers of all sorts, from touts to computer services available.

Unlike pro football, where the home field advantage is a constant 3, in the NBA it can move dramatically higher, all the way up to a 6 or beyond.

Basketball is really a contact sport as played in the NBA, and contact is punishable by the rules of the sport. Therefore, its all discretionary with the officials, and officials generally give the home team the benefit of the doubt. That's one of the reason overwhelming number of home court teams win their games. Other reasons involve the home crowd and the weariness of the visiting team.

This home court factor has to be carefully weighed on any given day.

OTHER HANDICAPPING FACTORS

TRAVEL

With an 82 game schedule, with teams constantly going from city to city, sometimes clear across the United States, travel is a definite factor in the NBA, and fatigue from travel must be taken into consideration when handicapping any game..

A team that's been on the road for awhile, especially when that's over-scheduled, with four game in six nights, for example, will show signs of fatigue. By the end of the road trip they may be tired and hurting.

This is even more the case when the team isn't a contender for the playoffs and has been losing games on the road. It may just play a weary sort of ball, not going after rebounds, not running up and won the court, just giving in.

When a road weary team is playing a fresh home team that is known for its speed, then that might be a good spot to put in a bet, expecting a blowout.

Some teams will perform fairly well on the road, if they're properly motivated. If a team needs a win to remain in the fight for a playoff spot, it will try hard no matter what the scheduling or where its playing. Motivation to win is a tremendous factor in any sport, and always go with the motivated team. It will fight like hell, and your bet won't go down easily.

INJURIES

Injuries become a major factor as the season wears on. Some players are always getting injured, and some great careers have been cut short as a result. That was true in the case of Bill Walton. Others, like Kareem Abdul-Jaabbar, were supremely conditioned athletes who could play season after season, game after game without any serious injury.

The game is a tough one, played on a hard wood court, and it is brutal on the legs. Also with all the contact, sometimes approaching wrestling under the boards, there are other injuries and all sorts of painful dislocations and bruises. The game takes its toll on nearly everyone who plays it in the NBA

The bookies take injuries into account when making the line. What is important to note is the type of player who is injured. If it's a shooter, then another shooter can take his place. The NBA is loaded with gunners who can come off the bench and hit the eyes out of a basket. However, if it is a strong body that is there for rebounds, that player may not be so quickly replaced.

Some teams depend on one player to such an extent that they're lost without him. This has become the case with the Lakers and Magic Johnson, or the Bulls and Michael Jordan.

No one is going to take the place of these already legendary ballplayers.

However, when they're out of the lineup, you've got to carefully study the line to see if you can make a bet either way, either against the team with the injury, taking the points, or going the other way, and laying points, figuring that the injured team just can't cut the mustard that night.

DRUGS

The NBA is full of high paid athletes who can shrug off a fine in the thousands of dollars, for after all, their pay is in the millions of dollars. With all that money available, with all the drugs available, it is no wonder that some of the NBA athletes use drugs. It's very difficult to keep up with the brutal schedule and the traveling, with the constant grid of play, having to be up night after night, playing at one's best.

Athletes have tried drugs like cocaine to give them that lift. It's reached a point in the NBA, where random drug testing is now mandatory. After a player has failed a few drug tests, he's out for life. That's a harsh penalty, but the NBA desperately wants to keep its image clean.

With drug testing, a few athletes of addictive personalities will still take a chance and use them, but the clubs are really careful about this these days. A tell-tale sign is the player who fades late in the game. It may be just fatigue, but if he performs like Superman the first half and like a dead dog the second, drugs may be suspect.

E. The Playoffs

The playoff season is really another season in the NBA. It starts after the regular season ends, and goes all the way to the middle of June. First, there is the best of 5 series, then the rest are best of seven. Then there's the title series.

In the playoffs, usually at the outset, form holds up well. The best of five matchups, with the better club having three home games to the weaker club's two, is sometimes a joke, with the better clubs sweeping all the games.

However, where there are no really dominant teams, these early games may become struggles, Sometimes there's an occasional upset.

After these games, when the best of seven approaches, they are usually fought hard, with the winner going to the conference championships. By this time, in the conference championships, we have two good teams playing.

The pressure is great, and sometimes a team can't sustain top play game after game. I've seen gamblers make money by betting against the team that won the previous game in these championship games.

However, don't blindly bet them. Study the situation carefully. If a team has struggled to get there, and has to play at its best just to get in a close win, then go against the club after it has struggled to a win. It probably has to regroup for the next game, and rest awhile.

In the finals, you again have to weigh the relative strengths of the two teams. Injuries play an important role here. If a key player is injured or doubtful, that may be all that is necessary to sink that team. A good example was the absence of Magic Johnson in the 1989 finals against Detroit, where the Pistons swept by Los Angeles for the title.

8. BETTING ON COLLEGE BASKETBALL

A. INTRODUCTION

Unlike the NBA, where there are 27 teams covered thoroughly by the media and the publications which devote themselves to pro basketball, out there in America are some 160 colleges which are able to field a team and therefore about eighty games a week which a gambler can wager on.

A bettor can have a good idea of how the Lakers or Pacers or Warriors or 76ers are stacking up for the going season, but what about Alabama-Birmingham, Ball State, Central Michigan, Virginia Tech, Toledo or St. Peter's?

It really is impossible to keep up with all of these obscure teams without some kind of guide. A good one is the *Gold Sheet*, which gives a constant rundown of the college teams. Or you can make up your own guide and records.

Bookmakers are very leery about college games, especially those involving small-time, rather than the big-time schools. They're afraid of making the wrong line, of not knowing the injuries or even the potential strength of the teams involved, and they're afraid of point-shaving or dumping of games for profit by college athletes.

In *Wiseguy*, the book about Mafia operations involving the crew of Paul Vario in New York, Henry Hill goes into detail about point-shaving at Boston University, a respected school in Massachusetts. He's blown the whistle on that situation, but are there

179

other situations around the country one doesn't hear about? Who knows?

In the big-time schools, the players, if they excel, expect to make it to the pros, to the big money in the NBA, and even if they don't get there, there are European teams beckoning with large contracts.

But for the average player on a backwater team, a player who might have come out of poverty, or just wants extra money, there can be a quick enticement by a gambler who tells him, "look, you don't have to throw the game, just shave off some points. So your team is favored by 12, well, you can win the game, but by fewer points. Your team will still win and there'll be a few hundred in it for you. Who's getting hurt but some gamblers and bookies? And best of all, how can anything be proved?"

In many cases, a bookmaker will not accept a bet over $500 on any college game. In Las Vegas, with all of their sports books functioning, much bigger money can be bet on a game. A lot of times, individual games may simply be taken off the boards, that is, no line established, or if a line had been made, no bets accepted.

This doesn't mean the game is fixed; it may simply mean that there are rumors of injuries, or something happened where the bookies can't really get a handle on the game, and are worried that their line is completely wrong.

B. KEEPING RECORDS

Like baseball betting, you've got to keep a lot of records when betting on the college buckets. You can't really follow 160 teams as well as you can twenty or thirty of them. That would be your best bet.

Follow a couple of conferences, or independent schools, but know them thoroughly. Feel that your line is better than the bookie's, and that you know more than he does. If you don't, you're not going to make money.

Don't just play hunches, bet intelligently.

Your records should show not only the straight-up won-lost records of the schools, but their records against the spread both home and away. It should show how they did as favorites and how they performed as dogs, both home and away.

If possible, get hold of the home town papers of the schools you're following. Find out about the school papers and see if you can subscribe to them. A lot of times they'll give you real information and an insight into how the squad feels. After all, in college basketball, there are only about six key players to think about when making a bet. Unlike the pros, where an NBA team may have All-Americans on the bench, in the college game, after the starters, the team generally slides way down in strength.

C. Analyzing the Game

Evaluating Coaches

A coach, such as Jim Valvano at North Carolina State in the eyes of some experts, simply didn't use his talent correctly, but played favorites. This would have been good information to know. He recruited well, but didn't use the talent wisely.

Generally, if you study the recruitment policies of a coach, that will give you an idea of how well the team will perform. With a good recruiting year, the team may be loaded with talent, eight deep, for example.

Is the coach playing all eight? If not, he may be, like so many college coaches, just another mediocrity, playing favorites. Or there may be dissension on the team.

If the coach can't get along with this players, and is a mere martinet, then go against this team. It'll get even with its coach by not trying hard enough. Or if the coach plays his starting five till they drop, that's another bad sign This is a coach who will try to win at all costs. Forget about the concerns of the athletes. That's secondary. The big W is all important. With a coach like this driving the squad, you can be sure that near the end of the season, the team will be ragged and worn-out, and then will fade quickly in the NCAA playoffs.

Coaches move around a lot; and have little loyalty to the school or the athletes they have recruited. For most of them, it's the almighty buck they worship, and if School A beckons with a bigger contact and more perks, School B is left in the dust, contract or no contract. Watch the coaches who are disloyal in this way. The first year or two they're all gung ho, but then they're looking for greener pastures.

Watch as their teams disintegrate. Look for those spots.

Coaches are ultimately responsible for the potential strength of their teams. In the pros, the players are kings. and a player like Magic Johnson can force out his coach, Paul Westhead. But in the college ranks, the coach is the boss, and he can make or break a team.

RATING THE TEAMS

Once you've decided on the number of schools you want to follow, you should rate them according to strength. Now, before we proceed any further, the schools followed and rated should be meeting each other during the season, or else there's no point in rating them. You don't want to follow Brown and CAl-Fullerton if they don't meet.

That's why we suggest following a few conferences, where the clubs will be playing each other. It could be the Big East or the WAC or the Big Eight, or whatever. The schools you follow should become very familiar to you- you should be comfortable betting on them because you know so much about them.

Give the best school a rating of 0, and work your way down, rating according to the point differential between them. For example, in the Big Eight, if you rank Oklahoma as a 0, and Kansas as a 3, then the Sooners are theoretically 3 points better than the JayHawks.

An Iowa State may be ranked as 14, which means that when State plays Kansas, you figure that Kansas is 11 points better than Iowa State (14-3).

Unless schools from different conferences play each other, you might want to keep separate records and rating for each individual conference.

In the Big Eight, it might look like this at the top:

Oklahoma	0
Kansas	3
Missouri	5

While, in the Big Ten, it might look like this:

Indiana	0
Michigan St	4
Ohio St.	5

There may come a time, in the playoffs or sometimes during the regular season, when these clubs play each other. If you anticipate this, during the season you will give a respective power rating to the Conferences themselves.

You might rate the Big Eight as 3 points better than the Big Ten, by studying their previous matchups. Or you might now start a separate rating, rating Oklahoma against Michigan St. if they should meet. It would look like this:

Oklahoma	0
Michigan St.	7

Once you've made your ratings, you can easily make up a line based on strength.

HOME COURT ADVANTAGE

To refine your line even more, you must give each team a home court advantage, expressed in points. To do this, you have to follow the teams from year to year. You might first have to look at the complete records of the teams from the previous year, seeing how well they performed at home, how they covered there.

Have the bookies given them too few or too many points as a

home court favorite? Or underdog?

Again, keeping and studying records is important. It's a complex task. If you want to make money, don't take the easy way out - study and put down as much information as you can - information that will help you make the right decision when placing your bets.

The *Gold Sheet* has a complete Home Court Value system. Study it for a quick fix and see if you agree with it, if it works for you. If it dows, then it will save you a lot of time. If it doesn't, then back to the drawing board.

TRAVEL

Although the college teams don't travel around as much as the pros, due to a much shorter season, they can get just as weary after a long road trip. And as in the pros, the home court officials favor the home team. That has to be figured in with the advantage we discussed before for the home squad.

Travel may not always be a factor, but in the cold weather, if a plane is delayed, if the players haven't had much rest or sleep and you have this information, go against the team that's fatigued.

DRUGS

Drugs have swept America and created a problem for all walks of society, and it's no different in the colleges. And among the basketball teams. Boosters and backers and other groups pour illegal money into the hands of top college basketball athletes. Crooked agents keep feeding them money.

Money buys a lot of things - sports car, gold chains and sometimes drugs. They're available, they're expensive but they can be bought.

Watch for this factor when you watch a game. Watch for the athlete who falls apart near the end of the game, whose point production disappears in the last quarter. Always be alert for this situation. A team on drugs in not a team you want to wager on.. A team like this may have a fantastic game and then a dead game. Look for this lack of consistency as evidence of possible drug use.

D. THE NCAA AND NIT
PLAYOFF TOURNAMENTS

Television, which as influenced so much of American sports, has made the NCAA tournament to determine the national champion, one of the big sporting events of the year. The hype that surrounds this event is enormous.

First, 64 teams are selected from around the country.

The conference champion are naturally picked as are the winners of conference tournaments set up for the purpose of getting into the NCAA.

Thus, a team in the Atlantic Coast Conference, a strong basketball powerhouse, with a mediocre record during the season, and perhaps placed fifth in the overall conference standings, can still make it to the NCAA tournament if it wins the ACC tournament at the end of the regular season.

Then a host of independent schools of indifferent rankings are picked. The criterion usually is 20 or more victories during the season, but even this isn't standard.

There are four regions, within which schools are seeded from 1 to 16. The regions are randomly selected, and a team from the East may be playing in the Western Regional.

Then it all boils down to the **Final Four**, where each of the schools that is selected gets close to a million dollars. It's big bucks fueling college sports today.

Then the ultimate winner is crowned the national champion. However, this school isn't necessarily the best team in the country. In recent years, Villanova, North Carolina State, Kansas and Michigan were national champions, yet none of them were the premier basketball team in the USA the year they won the title.

What is important to remember is that upsets abound in the NCAA tournament playoffs. Top ranked teams fall in the very first round, or squeak by some small school that nobody's ever heard about. Every year there's a Cinderella team moving towards the Final Four.

I believe money can be won simply by going with the dogs in

the opening rounds of play. Favorites fall quickly in this tournament. After all, these aren't pros, but college kids nervous about the spotlight. The big-time schools have everything to lose, and the lowest seeded teams have nothing to lose. And this makes for upsets galore! Study this angle; it'll make money for you.

The NIT gets the leftovers that the NCAA rejected. The finals are played in Madison Square Garden, while the earlier games are played as regional games. No longer can the Garden fill up with

these teams. The NIT is definitely a second-rate tournament. But if you 'have followed the teams playing there, you may have an edge over the bookies. By this time in the season, you would know a great deal about the different squads, and your line may very well be more accurate than the bookmaker's.

E. MONEY MANAGEMENT

Don't fall into the trap of betting too many games during the basketball season just because all that action is there. Bet sparingly, with one idea in mind, to win money.

That's all you should be interested in. And before you even bet cold cash, try part of the season making only mind bets. If you can't win doing this, don't think that betting real money will change anything. It will, but it'll only diminish your bankroll.

Be super-careful about your bankroll. Don't bet more than 2% of it on any one game. Limit the games. If you're able to win consistently, increase your percentage bets. Go up to 5% or even more, it it pays off.

But if you find yourself losing, decrease your bets. If you continue to lose, stop betting. See what you're doing wrong. Go back to mind bets, and see if you still lose. If you are, your line isn't any good. Study and restudy all the factors that have made up your line. What's wrong? Find the problem and correct it.

If you can't correct it, don't bet. And certainly never bet with money you can't afford to lose either financially or emotionally.

However, if your method of handicapping is correct, you can make a lot of money betting basketball. It's a long season, with a lot of action.

187

The Court Marshall™- Pro Basketball Super Program
$299.95 - IBM only

One of the **best-selling** of the Professor Jones software programs, this **strong-man strategy** is used by professional books such as Harrah's in Reno and the El Dorado to put out their widely circulated lines. This software is the real thing!

Pick Winners!

This incredible program is user programmable and can create countless scenarios to help you **pick winners!** The Court Marshall™regression analysis allows you to look at any of the previous games on a matchup to see emerging trends and score capability. For example, you can track home dogs that played as road dogs the last time out, or **whatever patterns you find profitable!**

Unlimited Patterns

You can create unlimited patterns and the Court Marshall™will alert you when they come up! **Two years** of statistics can be sorted through to find winning patterns, then these patterns or 'spot plays' can then be flagged in future games and bet accordingly.

Beat the Spread

Many customers have recorded **61% to 73% spread wins** using the Court Marshall. Your winning percentages can be increased by creating **more winning patterns.**

If you're a serious basketball betting enthusiast and want to get an edge on the bookie, don't make another bet without this winning strategy. The Court Marshall™will **give you the edge!**

Use the Court Marshall™to Win at Pro Basketball Betting!

Collegiate Football™- $149.95 (IBM, Apple, Macintosh, TRS, C/64)

This popular program contains the standard capabilities needed for college games, plus additional features that provide for even more powerful college football analysis.

A Powerful Winning Approach

This **enhanced package** generates Team Strength Ratings and Power Play results based on W/L ratios, consecutive losses and Home Field Advantage so that "ripe" opportunities can be isolated.

A unique feature of this well-thought out program is the 'second opinion' option of choosing cumulative weekly totals and then a *third look* by using a statistical analysis of one year's statistics!

Fast Results - Easy-to-Use

Input time for most handicappers averages only 20 minutes weekly for 100 teams!Like the other Professor Jones products, this package comes complete with a full, professionally done manual and Professor Jones full product support!

Win at College Football

Choose the teams you want to follow, and the Collegiate Football™software program will give you both a cumulative and multiple analysis to help you pick winners!

Beat the Bookie and Friends at College Football Betting!

Gold Lottery/Lotto™ - Only $49.95 -IBM, Apple, Mac, C64

The results of Professor Jones **extensive research** and development efforts in Lottery/Lotto analysis have come together! With **powerful features** and number handling ability, this **comprehensive** program represents a very **advanced tool** in lottery/lotto analysis and number prediction.

Many Winning Program Features

You can analyze up to 25 two digit numbers , from 1-80, use a Cluster Analysis (statistical method of determining which number has the highest probability of coming up after another certain number has been drawn).

Many Powerful Features

You don't need to know the technical terms (such as the Central Tendency and Linear Regression Analysis - though our manual will show you), but these techniques will take and analyze various factors to determine **winning numbers**. It even allows you to enter the degree of freedom to **control accuracy** and the range of numbers!

Clear, Easy-to-Read Output

The latest ideas and most successful approaches have been developed into one lottery and lotto analysis program and like all the other Professor Jones products, the output is given in easy-to-read numeric charts and graphs.

Much More

Complete documentation and examples are provided to start you analyzing Lotteries and Lottos quickly and successfully!

Be a Winner! Go for the Gold

Platinum Lottery/Lotto™ - $149.95 -IBM and Mac only

The Platinum is the king of the Lottery/Lotto software, and though the Gold is **powerful** and brings **excelent results**, this **powerhouse strategy** is selling at an increasing rate as well, for the Platinum Lottery/Lotto˜ is for players going for the max!

Why?

Super Strategy

This **super strategy** features over 20 of the Dimitrov Systems, the Hard Positional Analysis, all the cluster, Bell, % of Occurrence, % of Frequency, Past Winning Numbers, two digit numbers and a lot more!

The Platinum Lottery/Lotto™also features an expanded cluster analysis, skip hit chart, hot number analysis, regression analysis and unlimited wheeling systems. Very powerful - an excellent top-of-the-line strategy!

Be a Winner! Go for the platinum!

Customers have enjoyed success with both the Gold and the Platinum - its up to you to choose which you feel is more appropriate for your needs. The Gold Strategy is excellent for beginning level Lotto and Lottery players and is one of Professor Jones best deals at $49.95, while the Platinum Strategy addresses experienced intermediate and advanced players and is an excellent buy at $149.95.

Order the Lottery/Lotto Strategy's Today!

The Gambling Maniac's Diary

This fun diary is beautifully bound in a gold-stamped, non-rip, kivar cover, is a handy 3 3/4 x 7" and contains 176 pages of *everything* for you lovers of gambling! Buy one for friends and family. The Gambling Maniac's Diary is a great gift!

The diary shows you **how to play and win** at eight of the most popular casino games and is generously illustrated with tables, charts and diagrams. There's even a **money management** chapter to help you come home with the money you've won!

And now **the fun begins.** Every week in the diary section, alongside your daily planner, we present some wild ideas in the gamble of the week. For example, when is the last time you bet on where a fly will land or how many bites out of a sandwich a person will take! **It's all here!**

Find out how your upcoming year looks in the Gambling Maniac's **Horoscope** section and test your wits and gambling knowledge against our **quizzes** and **crossword.** Or check out the **World Casino Guide** section (worth $10 by itself!) and find out where the gambling action is around the world! We leave room for you to keep your more important names and addresses, and the diary even shows how to play the most fun gamble of them all - **strip poker!**

All in all, for you gambling maniac's and lovers, here's a great place to record your year!!! All this for **only $10!**

The Oddsmaker

This is the **important reference** book every gambler must have! The Oddsmaker is Gambling Research Institute's **definitive** work and **complete guide** to the odds at all the casino games. You name the game and the Oddsmaker will tell you where you stand against the house! **Tons of information** in this valuable book for **only $10!**

The Basics of Gambling

This **enormously popular** boxed set is back again in a **new, exciting** edition - a shrink-wrapped boxed set in **money green** and emblazoned with a **gold star** - it makes a great gift item! This **beautiful set** contains five individual books that show how to play and win at five of the most popular gambling pursuits and includes, *The Basics of Blackjack, The Basics of Craps, The Basics of Poker, The Basics of Horseracing* and the *Basics of Roulette.*

750,000 people have bought books from this series. They can't all be wrong! **Just $15!**

-Our Complete Catalogue Sent Free With All Orders-

Van - Paul's
Winning Football Bettor - $50.00

Van Paul has studied the ins and outs of sports betting for most of his 55 years, and besides being one of the most knowledgeable sports bettors alive, Van Paul has been a **consistent winner**, and this **super-strategy** will show how you can be a **winner** too!

Debunks the Myths

Before anything else Van-Paul clears the air. He shows why there is no such thing as a lock, and why you should **use your own winning strategies.** This section alone is worth the price of the strategy for you'll never buy a tout sheet again after reading **Van Paul's Five Tier Safeguard Play.** But let's move on to the meat and potatoes.

Beat the Spread

There are many good handicapping philosophies out there and many factors you use to get that edge, but somehow you find, you really don't have that edge - that you're losing. Lose no more! This strategy will give you that "little extra," and **make you a winner!**

The Weather Key

Van Paul's secret key to winning lies in finding the **sweet spots.** We all know how weather conditions - wind, glaring heat, rain, snow, extreme cold, humidity, fog and other conditions can influence the outcome of a game, but how many of us know how to *really* use these factors?

Well, Van Paul has studied and **won with this strategy** for more than 20 years - and you know something, the principles don't change!

Step by Step Guide

There are many important and valuable points to making maximum use of this strategy, so Van Paul lays out his strategy **point by point,** showing how certain *types of teams* react under different weather conditions. For instance, the weather is turning nasty, and the teams will be playing in the bitter cold. How do you adjust your line? Which teams can you make a profit betting on?

Learn How to Win

You'll **learn how to win** at games that to others, seem on the surface, to be fairly even, but armed with Van Paul's **inside winning strategies,** you'll see that in reality, they're not balanced and you have a big edge against the line! Van Paul will show you how to find the teams and players that will win in the sun, others that just won't hold up when the weather turns cold.

The Hidden Edge

This in-depth study gives you a **whole new look on winning,** showing you when to go against the flow and where your best bets are. You'll learn how to analyze the key players and positions, the key trends and all the other important factors *in relation to the weather!*

It's Time to Win

How many times have bets you felt were good go down the tubes and loss after devastating loss sink your bankroll? No more. You've been overlooking perhaps the most important Handicapping factor - **The Weather Key.**

Now this information is available **for the first time**, and can be yours to get that **extra edge** you've always needed to **make you a winner!**

Bonus

With your order, you'll receive, **absolutely free,** *Van Paul's Underdog Best Play Pick's* ($10 Value) - a winning guide that gives you an **extra winnig edge.**
Order the "Winning Football Bettor" Today!